THRIVE

SELF-IMPROVEMENT STRATEGIES FOR NEW MANAGERS

ANTHONY HUTTON

ST. JAMES PRESS

To my dearest mother, whose unwavering strength and wisdom light my path, and to my sister Paula, whose resilience and compassion inspire me daily. This journey, imprinted with your love and guidance, is a testament to our enduring bond.

Leadership and learning are indispensable to each other.

— JOHN F. KENNEDY

CONTENTS

PREFACE

JOURNEY INTO MANAGEMENT: TRANSITION FROM TEAM MEMBER TO MANAGER

The leap from team member to manager is akin to setting sail on uncharted waters, filled with both exhilaration and the unknown. It's a journey that transforms not just your title but also the core of your professional identity. Picture yourself at the helm, where once you rowed in sync with others, now guiding the ship's course.

This transition is a mosaic of new responsibilities and nuanced relationships. Gone are the days when your success hinged solely on your individual efforts. Now, you're sculpting a team's destiny; your hands are molding a collective vision. It's about nurturing a garden of diverse talents where your growth is intertwined with the flourishing of others.

Yet, this journey isn't a linear path from point A to point B. It's a spiral staircase, where each step elevates your perspective, revealing new horizons. With every challenge comes the chance to stretch your wings and discover facets of leadership you never knew existed. It's an odyssey of self-discovery, where the lessons are as unique as the individuals undertaking them.

THE PURPOSE OF THIS BOOK: GOALS AND READER EXPECTATIONS

This book is a compass in your hands, designed to guide you through the labyrinth of management. It's a lighthouse, shining light on the complexities and joys of leading. We aim to arm you with tools, techniques, and wisdom to navigate the multifaceted roles you'll embody.

Expect this journey through the pages to be enlightening, sometimes challenging, but always rewarding. Each chapter is crafted as a stepping stone, incrementally building your skills and understanding. We'll explore the tangible aspects of management, sure, but also the intangible—the art of leadership—that textbooks often overlook.

This book is an interactive journey, bridging the gap between your ambitions and our expertise. Rather than merely offering answers, we aim to ignite thought-provoking questions that drive you toward profound understanding. Each page offers a fusion of practical strategies and reflective insights, catering to both the emerging manager and the experienced leader. Expect a narrative that delves deep into the nuances of management, equipping you with a toolbox of techniques and perspectives to navigate your professional path.

THE ROLE OF SELF-IMPROVEMENT IN MANAGEMENT: IMPORTANCE OF CONTINUOUS GROWTH

In the dynamic world of management, remaining static is tantamount to regressing. The business environment is in constant flux, making continuous self-improvement not just advantageous but necessary. Picture it as caring for a garden —the more attention and care you give it, the more it flourishes.

This journey of ongoing growth is like weaving a tapestry with threads of new abilities, experiences, and reflective insights. It's about understanding that each obstacle is a stepping stone to a greater comeback, and every hurdle presents an opportunity to enhance your comprehension. As a manager, you are perpetually a learner and a mentor, consistently evolving and always striving to surpass your past self.

Yet, self-enhancement is not a lone endeavor. It flourishes amidst the richness of collective experiences and varied viewpoints. It involves heeding the subtle lessons in each triumph and setback, whether they are your own or others. This journey is a nuanced dance of acquiring and shedding knowledge, a delicate equilibrium of staying true to your core principles while remaining receptive to novel concepts.

NAVIGATING THE OUTLINE: HOW TO USE THIS BOOK EFFECTIVELY

Consider this book as your personal roadmap to management mastery. It's structured to guide you, step by step, through the intricate dance of leadership. But like any journey, the magic lies not in the destination but in the journey itself. Dive into each chapter not just with the intent to learn but also to engage and reflect.

To navigate this outline effectively, approach each chapter as a new adventure. Let the subheadings be your guideposts, each a window into a critical management aspect. They're not just topics but invitations to explore and delve deeper into the art and science of leading.

But don't rush. Savor each section, chew on the ideas, and digest them at your own pace. This isn't a race; it's a journey of enrichment. Each paragraph and each sentence is crafted to build upon the last, weaving a tapestry of knowledge that grows richer with every page turned. And remember, the true value lies not just in reading but in applying these insights to your unique situation.

INTRODUCTION

UNDERSTANDING THE NEW MANAGER'S LANDSCAPE: CHALLENGES AND OPPORTUNITIES

Entering the realm of management is akin to navigating through a dense, uncharted woodland. The trail is often obscured and laden with unforeseen challenges. As a manager, you'll confront various trials, from harmonizing a diverse team to achieving ambitious organizational objectives. Yet, within each challenge lies a veiled chance for growth, innovation, and discovering hidden strengths. By confronting these difficulties, you carve new pathways to success, transforming each hurdle into a foundation for advancement.

The environment of a new manager is interspersed with illuminating opportunities, like clearings in the forest where the sky is visible. These moments present chances to demonstrate your capabilities, significantly impact your team, and effect meaningful change within the organization. Seizing these opportunities demands bravery and foresight, but the outcomes are profoundly rewarding.

This landscape is in constant flux, necessitating a mix of adaptability and steadfastness. As a manager, you need to be responsive to the shifting dynamics of the organization while upholding your fundamental values and vision. This requires a balance akin to being as resilient as an oak and as flexible as a willow. Mastering this equilibrium is central to adept management, where the goal transcends mere survival and encompasses thriving and flourishing.

ESSENTIAL QUALITIES OF EFFECTIVE MANAGERS: KEY ATTRIBUTES

Imagine a manager as a skilled sailor navigating the vast ocean of the workplace. Certain qualities are indispensable to steer the ship successfully. Foremost among these is emotional intelligence - the ability to understand and manage one's own emotions and those of others. This skill is like the compass that guides the ship, ensuring you navigate the human aspects of the workplace with empathy and understanding.

Another key attribute is effective communication. It's the wind in your ship's sails, propelling you forward. A good manager communicates clearly and listens actively, creating an environment where ideas flow freely and everyone feels heard. This skill fosters collaboration and builds trust, essential components for any successful team.

Strategic thinking is also vital. It's the map that guides your journey, helping you plot a course that aligns with the organization's goals while navigating through challenges. This involves not only setting clear objectives but also antici-pating and mitigating risks. It's about seeing beyond the horizon and preparing for what's to come.

THE IMPORTANCE OF SELF-AWARENESS: BUILDING A GROWTH FOUNDATION

Being an adept manager fundamentally hinges on robust self-awareness, like a ship's stabilizing keel that ensures it remains upright amid turbulent waters. Recognizing your own strengths, acknowledging your weaknesses, and under-standing your biases and blind spots are essential. This profound awareness forms the bedrock of your leadership style, anchoring your decisions and interactions in a sincere understanding of who you are.

Embarking on the journey of self-discovery is comparable to excavating the layers of an ancient city; each level uncovered offers more profound insights into your character, values, and how you engage with the world. It necessitates reflection and often the courage to face uncomfortable truths about oneself. Yet, this deep dive into your psyche is invaluable, enabling you to lead authentically and honestly.

The pursuit of self-awareness is continuous, much like the ongoing work of a gardener nurturing their garden. It demands consistent cultivation—seeking feedback, reflecting on experiences, and being receptive to lessons from both successes and failures. In this ever-expanding garden of self, growth is constant, and the fruits it bears are essential for compassionate and effective leadership.

EMBRACING CHANGE AND ADAPTABILITY: STAYING RELEVANT

Change is an ever-present management aspect, much like the ocean's ever-changing tides. To maintain relevance and effectiveness, a manager must embody adaptability, molding themselves to new circumstances just as water fits into any shape. This entails embracing fresh ideas, being flexible in strategy, and being prepared to shift direction as needed.

Being adaptable is more than just a reactive measure; it's about actively seeking and welcoming novel methods and practices. It's comparable to a dancer who fluidly moves with the changing beats of the music. Such agility enables a manager to guide their team through changes seamlessly, transforming potential challenges into opportunities for development and creative solutions.

However, adapting to change transcends mere skill; it's an attitude. It involves the readiness to abandon old ways and the eagerness to delve into new prospects. It's fostering a culture where change is not seen as a threat but as a driving force for enhancement. In a world that's constantly evolving, adaptability becomes an invaluable asset, ensuring that both you and your team don't just endure but flourish.

SETTING PERSONAL AND PROFESSIONAL GOALS: ROADMAP TO SUCCESS

As a manager, setting goals is like plotting a course for an extensive journey. These objectives serve as your guiding star, navigating you through the intricacies of management and ensuring alignment with your overarching vision. They offer both direction and inspiration, aiding you in steering through obstacles and recognizing your triumphs.

Personal objectives are centered on self-enhancement – refining your leadership abilities, broadening your expertise, and cultivating emotional intelligence. These goals are the milestones that signify your evolution as a leader, comparable to notable landmarks along a voyage. They serve as reminders of the progress you've made and fuel your drive to continue advancing.

Conversely, professional goals pertain to the impact you aspire to achieve in your position. They encompass elevating team performance, fostering innovation, and contributing to your organization's overall success. These ambitions act as guiding lights in the darkness, casting a luminous trail toward shared success and gratification.

THE ROLE OF MENTORSHIP AND LEARNING: LEARNING FROM OTHERS

Within the intricate weave of management, mentorship and ongoing learning stand out as dynamic and enriching elements. Mentorship acts as a beacon, shedding light on the journey ahead with insights and lessons from those who have previously navigated similar paths. It offers a fresh perspective, valuable understanding, and the motivation needed to traverse the complexities of management with increased assurance.

Learning is a continual journey in both its formal and informal forms. It's like steadily adding diverse tools to your arsenal, with each new skill or nugget of knowledge enhancing your proficiency as a manager. This could include participating in workshops, delving into industry publications, or gleaning insights from the everyday challenges of leading a team.

However, the significance of mentorship and learning transcends individual growth. It's about cultivating an ethos of continuous development within your team. You foster a workspace where learning is encouraged and a shared endeavor by encouraging team members to seek mentors, remain inquisitive, and persistently refine their abilities. This approach nurtures an environment where the pursuit of knowledge and skill is not just an individual quest but a collective journey embraced by all.

ESTABLISHING A PERSONAL LEADERSHIP STYLE: CRAFTING UNIQUENESS

Crafting your personal leadership style is similar to creating your own signature piece of art. It's an intricate mix of your individual traits, life experiences, core values, and skills, all coming together to form a leadership approach that's unmistakably yours. This distinctive style influences how you guide your team and the mark you leave on your organization.

Like a river continuously shaping its course, your leadership style isn't fixed; it evolves. It changes as a result of the various difficulties you face, the criticism you take in, and the knowledge you gain along the way. This evolution is a dynamic process, constantly adjusting and refining itself.

Discovering your unique leadership approach is a process of trial and error. It involves experimenting with various methods and figuring out what aligns and what doesn't, all while staying true to your essence. Authenticity is critical; your style should echo your deepest values and beliefs. It's this genuineness that fosters trust and respect within your team.

Developing your leadership style is a continual journey that demands self-awareness, the ability to adapt, and a commitment to personal growth. Embark on this path with an open and willing spirit, and witness the gradual unveiling of your distinctive leadership style, steering you towards the leader you're meant to become.

BUILDING EFFECTIVE
COMMUNICATION SKILLS

LISTENING WITH EMPATHY: UNDERSTANDING
TEAM NEEDS

L istening empathetically as a manager is much like being a discerning gardener who carefully tends to the specific needs of each plant. It involves delving into the finer points of your team's communication, capturing both the spoken words and the unspoken elements. This level of listening extends beyond mere words to grasp the essence of the speaker's emotions and thoughts. It elevates typical exchanges to deep, significant conversations, forging a bond of comprehension and trust.

Empathetic listening means fully immersing yourself in the conversation with an open heart and mind, putting aside personal biases and preconceptions. It's about being wholly present and offering your complete focus to the person speaking. Such attentive listening ensures team members feel truly heard and appreciated, promoting inclusion and mutual respect.

Yet, practicing empathetic listening also demands keen self-awareness. It requires acknowledging your own perspectives and emotions, ensuring they don't skew your understanding of the message being conveyed. Think of it as a duet with two distinct but complementary voices. Each vocalist must listen and adjust to the other, blending their tones and pitches in perfect harmony while also ensuring their individual voice remains clear and true. This delicate balance of unity and distinctiveness creates a beautiful and cohesive melody, far richer than either could achieve alone. This approach doesn't just solidify team bonds; it deepens your insight into each team member's individual viewpoints.

Moreover, empathetic listening within a team is a continuous endeavor, not just a singular action. It calls for consistent interactions and open dialogues, nurturing a culture where feedback is welcomed and sought after. By cultivating such an atmosphere, you address present concerns and proactively prepare for future challenges, setting the stage for a more unified and forward-thinking team.

ARTICULATING VISION AND EXPECTATIONS: CLEAR MESSAGING

Conveying your vision and expectations is like sketching out a detailed map for a treasure hunt, where clarity paves the way to triumph. It involves formulating a message that strikes a chord with your team and guides and inspires them. A clearly communicated vision forges a unified objective, aligning individual contributions with the organization's broader goals.

When you communicate your vision, it's not just the words that count but the zeal and conviction behind them. Your enthusiasm for the vision becomes infectious, igniting a similar zeal within your team. It's like painting a vivid and compelling portrait of the future that energizes and propels your team forward.

Yet, achieving clarity in conveying your vision and expectations also hinges on consistency. Your actions and decisions should mirror the ideals and objectives you promote. Such consistency fortifies trust and credibility, rendering your vision more concrete and achievable for your team.

Moreover, sharing your vision is not just about speaking; it's equally about listening. It involves valuing your team's feedback and viewpoints and being open to adjusting your strategy accordingly. This reciprocal dialogue ensures that your vision is understood and collectively embraced and championed by the entire team.

FEEDBACK DYNAMICS: GIVING AND RECEIVING FEEDBACK

Mastering feedback dynamics is like navigating a complex dance where every step and turn is crucial. When you give constructive feedback, you provide guidance and support, helping your team members grow and improve. It's about delivering your message clearly but compassionately, ensuring that it's received as a tool for development rather than criticism.

Receiving feedback is equally important in this dynamic. It requires humility and openness, recognizing that feedback is a gift that can lead to personal and professional growth. It's about listening actively, considering the feedback without defensiveness, and using it as a springboard for improvement.

Balancing the act of giving and receiving feedback requires emotional intelligence and tact. It's about knowing when to speak, what to say, and how to say it. This balance ensures that feedback becomes a positive force in your team, fostering a culture of continuous learning and development.

In addition, effective feedback dynamics involve creating an environment where feedback is not just accepted but encouraged and valued. It's about establishing regular opportunities for feedback, both formally and informally. This continuous communication loop ensures that your team remains aligned, engaged, and motivated.

NAVIGATING DIFFICULT CONVERSATIONS: MANAGING SENSITIVE TOPICS

Navigating difficult conversations is a crucial skill for any manager. It's about approaching sensitive topics with honesty, empathy, and tact. Often fraught with emotions, these conversations require a careful and thoughtful approach to ensure they lead to positive outcomes.

Managing difficult conversations also involves preparing thoroughly. Anticipate potential responses, plan your key points, and consider the best setting for the discussion. It's about being proactive rather than reactive, setting the stage for a constructive and respectful dialogue.

But it's not just about what you say but also how you say it. Your tone, body language, and choice of words can significantly impact how your message is received. Strive to communicate clearly, directly, sensitively, and respectfully, ensuring that the conversation remains focused and productive.

Moreover, navigating difficult conversations requires resilience and patience. These discussions may not always go as planned, and it's essential to remain calm and composed, even when faced with resistance or emotional responses. Maintaining your composure sets the tone for the conversation, steering it towards a constructive resolution.

CROSS-CULTURAL COMMUNICATION: EMBRACING DIVERSITY

In our increasingly globalized work environment, the significance of cross-cultural communication cannot be overstated. It revolves around recognizing and valuing the diverse backgrounds and perspectives that each team member contributes. This variety of experiences and viewpoints is an asset and a wellspring of innovation and creativity, enriching team discussions and outcomes.

Mastering cross-cultural communication involves maintaining an open mind and a readiness to absorb new information. It's about nurturing a curiosity for different cultures, engaging in thoughtful inquiries, and respecting varying viewpoints. Adopting this mindset promotes a team atmosphere that is both inclusive and cooperative.

Nevertheless, navigating cross-cultural communication comes with its own set of hurdles. Language barriers, distinct communication styles, and varying cultural norms can lead to misunderstandings. Recognizing and sensitively addressing these potential complications is crucial, requiring both awareness and flexibility.

Moreover, genuinely embracing diversity in communication extends beyond mere acceptance; it involves appreciating and valuing the unique insights and approaches that different cultures contribute to the team dynamic. Cultivating an environment where these differences are celebrated can significantly boost team unity, spur innovation, and fuel creative problem-solving.

COMMUNICATING IN A DIGITAL AGE: LEVERAGING TECHNOLOGY

Navigating communication in the digital era entails skillfully utilizing various technological tools. From the immediacy of emails and instant messaging to the interactive nature of video conferencing and the broad reach of social media, each channel offers its own distinct advantages and potential pitfalls. The key lies in selecting the most suitable platform for your message and ensuring that your communication remains clear and impactful, no matter the chosen medium.

Yet, digital communication often misses the subtleties inherent in face-to-face interactions. The absence of physical gestures and expressions means messages can be easily misinterpreted. Therefore, paying extra attention to your tone and choice of words in digital formats is crucial, ensuring sufficient context and clarity.

However, the digital landscape also opens up creativity and innovative communication possibilities. It enables immediate collaboration across different locations, breaking down geographical barriers. Leveraging these digital tools can significantly boost team collaboration and productivity, uniting team members in exciting and versatile ways.

In addition, adept communication in today's digital world also involves a solid grasp of digital etiquette. This means knowing when an email is more appropriate than a phone call, understanding how to use various platforms effectively, and respecting online boundaries. Mastering these subtleties ensures that your digital communications are efficient but also considerate and successful.

DEVELOPING A PERSONAL COMMUNICATION STYLE: AUTHENTICITY IN INTERACTION

Developing a personal communication style is about finding your voice as a leader. It's a style that reflects your personality, values, and leadership philosophy. This authenticity in communication builds trust and credibility, making your interactions more genuine and effective.

But finding your style doesn't happen overnight. It's a trial-and-error process, adapting and refining your approach based on feedback and experience. It's about being open to learning and growing and being willing to adjust your style as needed.

A personal communication style is also about balance. It's finding the right mix of professionalism, approachability, directness, and empathy. This balance ensures that your communication is effective across different contexts and audiences.

Finally, developing a personal communication style involves self-awareness. It's about understanding how your communication impacts others and being mindful of the messages you're sending verbally and non-verbally. By cultivating this level of self-awareness, you ensure that your communication style is authentic and resonates positively with your team.

TIME MANAGEMENT AND DELEGATION

PRIORITIZING TASKS: EFFECTIVE TASK MANAGEMENT

In management, prioritizing tasks is like being the conductor of an orchestra. The crucial aspect is to identify which instruments need to lead at which moments—the ones that bring harmony and coherence to the entire performance. It involves discerning which tasks demand immediate action and which ones can be deferred. Mastering this art of prioritization is critical to optimizing your time and resources and ensuring focus on activities that propel progress and success.

However, effective prioritization extends beyond merely listing tasks; it's about comprehending each duty's significance and potential impact. Assess the possible outcomes and risks linked to every task on your agenda. It's similar to strategizing in chess; you have to contemplate several steps ahead, foreseeing the ramifications of each move. This tactical method of prioritizing keeps you aligned with your long-term objectives while adeptly managing daily duties.

Prioritization in management also entails flexibility. Priorities may need to shift swiftly in reaction to fresh insights or evolving scenarios. Adapting and reprioritizing promptly is essential, much like a seasoned surfer who adjusts their approach with each new wave and shift in the wind.

Furthermore, intelligent task prioritization involves effective delegation. Identifying tasks that can be assigned to others can free up your schedule to concentrate on high-importance items that necessitate your specific skills. It's about entrusting your team with responsibilities and empowering them to take charge of their tasks.

THE ART OF DELEGATION: EMPOWERING TEAM MEMBERS

Mastering the art of delegation is essential for any effective manager. It's not merely about distributing tasks but empowering your team to take on new challenges and grow. Good delegation involves identifying and matching team members' strengths with suitable tasks. It's like a coach assigning positions to players to maximize the team's overall strength and cohesion.

However, effective delegation also requires clear communication. You must ensure that your team members understand what they must do and why it's important. This clarity helps them see the bigger picture and their role in achieving the team's goals. It's about painting a clear path they can follow that aligns with their skills and the team's objectives.

Additionally, delegation involves a degree of letting go. It means trusting your team to handle tasks without constant oversight. This trust is vital for their development and your ability to focus on higher-level strategic planning. It's like teaching someone to ride a bike; eventually, you must let go and trust them to pedal on their own.

Furthermore, effective delegation also includes providing the necessary resources and support. It's about setting your team up for success and ensuring they have the tools and guidance to complete their tasks effectively. This support reinforces their confidence and ability to tackle assigned responsibilities.

AVOIDING OVERCOMMITMENT: BALANCING WORKLOAD

Avoiding overcommitment is like finding the perfect balance in a well-choreographed dance. It requires knowing your limits and understanding the capacity of your team. Overcommitment can lead to burnout and decreased productivity, so it's crucial to recognize when to say no. It's about assessing each request or opportunity carefully, weighing its importance against your current commitments.

Managing workloads effectively also involves realistic planning. It's about setting achievable goals and deadlines, considering your team's capacity and resources. This realistic approach prevents the pitfalls of overcommitment and ensures that the quality of work is not compromised. It's like planning a journey; you must account for rest stops and potential delays to ensure a smooth trip.

One of the benefits of learning to delegate effectively is that doing so can help manage overcommitment. It's about understanding that you don't have to shoulder all the responsibilities yourself. Delegating tasks to capable team members can help distribute the workload more evenly.

Moreover, avoiding overcommitment also means being proactive in managing expectations. Communicate openly with your team and stakeholders about what can realistically be achieved. This transparency helps in setting realistic expectations and reduces the pressure of overcommitment.

STRATEGIES FOR EFFICIENT SCHEDULING: OPTIMIZING TIME

Efficient scheduling in management is like creating a well-oiled machine where every component works in harmony with the others. It involves organizing your tasks and responsibilities to maximize efficiency and minimize wasted time. Effective scheduling is about understanding the rhythm of your workday and aligning tasks with your most productive periods. It's like a chef planning the kitchen workflow to ensure each dish is prepared and served perfectly.

One effective strategy for efficient scheduling is time blocking, where specific blocks are dedicated to different tasks or types of work. This method can significantly enhance focus and productivity by reducing the constant switching between tasks, known as context switching. It's like compartmentalizing your day into segments, each dedicated to a specific purpose or goal.

Moreover, effective scheduling also requires flexibility. Unforeseen events and shifting priorities are a part of every manager's life. Being able to adapt your schedule on the fly without losing sight of your primary objectives is key. It's like being a skilled improviser in a jazz band, ready to change the tune as the rhythm dictates.

Additionally, prioritizing tasks within your schedule is crucial. It's about distinguishing between what needs immediate attention and what can be deferred. This prioritization ensures that critical tasks are addressed first and time is used as effectively as possible.

TOOLS FOR TIME MANAGEMENT: TECHNOLOGICAL AIDS

In today's digital world, various technological tools aid in time management. These tools, from calendar apps to project management software, act as your digital assistants, helping you organize, plan, and track your tasks and responsibilities. They are the scaffolding for building a more structured and efficient workday.

However, the key to effectively using these tools lies in selecting those that best fit your work style and needs. It's about finding the right tool that complements your workflow rather than complicating it. Think of it as choosing the right instrument to play a particular piece of music; the right tool can make the task at hand not only easier but also more enjoyable.

Moreover, while these technological aids are invaluable, they should not replace human judgment and adaptability. They are meant to supplement your skills, not supplant them. It's about using technology to enhance your efficiency, not dictate it.

Additionally, integrating these tools into your team's work-flow can enhance overall productivity and coordination. It involves creating a shared digital space where all team members can easily access and manage tasks and schedules.

CREATING BOUNDARIES: PERSONAL AND PROFESSIONAL BALANCE

Creating boundaries in time management is like drawing lines in the sand. It's about demarcating where your work ends and your personal life begins. This separation is crucial for maintaining a healthy work-life balance and preventing burnout. Setting boundaries might involve designated work hours, turning off work notifications after hours, or having specific days dedicated to uninterrupted work or rest.

However, establishing these boundaries can be challenging in an always-on digital world. Adherence to them requires discipline and commitment, even when the temptation to cross them is strong. It's like a gardener setting a fence around their garden; it protects the space from being overrun but requires regular maintenance.

Moreover, communicating these boundaries to your team and colleagues is essential. It sets expectations and fosters mutual respect for personal time. When everyone under-stands and respects these boundaries, it creates a healthier and more productive work environment.

Furthermore, it's important to reassess and adjust your boundaries periodically. As your personal and professional life evolves, so too might your need for different boundaries. Regularly reviewing and adjusting them ensures they continue to serve your best interests.

OVERCOMING PROCRASTINATION: MAINTAINING PRODUCTIVITY

Overcoming procrastination is like navigating through a maze in your own mind. It often requires deconstructing complex challenges into simpler, more navigable paths, making them feel less overwhelming. This method can transform a seemingly insurmountable obstacle into a sequence of manageable steps, like finding your way through a labyrinth, one turn at a time.

Implementing strict timelines and fostering a sense of immediacy can also ward off procrastination. Deadlines serve as catalysts, compelling you to initiate and conclude tasks within a specified period. It's comparable to a countdown that drives you onward, concentrating your attention squarely on the task at hand.

Yet, unraveling the underlying reasons for your procrastination is crucial. Be it a fear of failure, a quest for perfection, or a simple lack of enthusiasm, recognizing and addressing these root causes can pave the way for more effective strategies to counter procrastination and bolster productivity. It's akin to understanding the blueprint of a maze before attempting to navigate it.

Additionally, reframing your attitude towards tasks is part of overcoming procrastination. Seeing tasks as opportunities for advancement rather than burdensome chores can alter your perception and diminish the inclination to delay. It's about appreciating the journey of each task and relishing the sense of accomplishment that comes with its completion.

DEVELOPING EMOTIONAL INTELLIGENCE

UNDERSTANDING EMOTIONAL INTELLIGENCE: KEY COMPONENTS

Grasping Emotional Intelligence (EI) is comparable to mastering a new language that enhances your ability to interact with yourself and others more proficiently. It encompasses various skills, including the ability to identify and comprehend your own emotions and those of people around you. This insight acts as a navigational tool, steering your interactions and the way you make decisions. Recognizing emotions is the initial step, like discerning individual notes in a tune, which helps you grasp their impact on actions and communication.

The next element of EI involves reasoning with emotions. This is about utilizing your emotional insights to make informed and empathetic decisions. Imagine a chef who understands how each ingredient influences a dish's overall taste; similarly, this facet of EI enables you to foresee how emotions might affect various scenarios. It's the art of merging emotional insight with logical thinking to handle the intricate social dynamics at work adeptly.

Another crucial aspect of EI is the management of emotions. This skill is like a skilled juggler, expertly balancing multiple objects in the air. Just as the juggler must be aware of and control each item's trajectory and speed to maintain harmony and prevent chaos, managing your emotional reactions involves carefully balancing and regulating various emotional responses to maintain composure and ensure constructive outcomes. It's about controlling your emotions and reacting to situations with composure and poise. This self-regulation is vital in a professional environment where uncontrolled emotions can lead to conflicts or misunderstandings.

SELF-REGULATION AND MANAGEMENT: CONTROLLING IMPULSES

Self-regulation in the context of emotional intelligence is like having an internal thermostat; it's about knowing when to turn up the heat and when to cool down. This skill involves recognizing your emotional triggers and controlling your impulsive responses. It's the art of pausing before reacting, giving yourself time to assess the situation and respond in a way aligned with your goals and values.

Managing impulses is not about suppression; it's about conscious control. It's like being a skilled rider, knowing when to rein in your horse and when to let it gallop. This control enables you to navigate challenging situations without letting emotions take the reins, leading to more thoughtful and practical responses.

However, self-regulation also requires practice. It's a skill that improves over time with mindfulness and self-aware-ness. Regular reflection on your emotional responses and the situations that trigger them can help you develop stronger self-regulation skills. It's like exercising a muscle; the more you practice, the stronger it becomes.

Furthermore, self-regulation often involves changing habitual responses. It's about identifying patterns in your emotional reactions and actively working to modify them. This change can be challenging but essential for personal and professional growth. It's like charting a new course in uncharted waters—gloomy but ultimately rewarding.

EMPATHY IN LEADERSHIP: CONNECTING WITH OTHERS

Empathy in leadership serves as a conduit for comprehen-sion and rapport, much like a bridge linking two separate lands. It entails stepping into your team's shoes and grasping their viewpoints and emotions. This empathetic stance improves communication and cultivates a nurturing, collab-orative atmosphere within the team.

However, empathy extends beyond merely understanding others; it's also about visibly caring for them. It's akin to a comforting glow in a chilly environment, offering solace and assurance. Showing genuine concern can forge deeper trust and devotion, strengthening the bond between you and your team members.

In resolving conflicts, empathy is invaluable. By grasping the emotions and viewpoints of all involved, you can approach disagreements with sensitivity and fairness. It's comparable to being a wise mediator who comprehends the entire situation, assisting in reaching a solution that respects everyone's feelings and necessities.

Furthermore, empathy contributes to more sound decision-making. By weighing the emotional implications of your decisions on your team, you can make effective but also kind and considerate choices. It's about harmonizing the logical with the emotional, ensuring comprehensive and thoughtful decisions.

BUILDING RELATIONSHIP SKILLS: FOSTERING STRONG BONDS

Nurturing relationships in the workplace is akin to cultivating a garden; it demands time, dedication, and attentive care. The roots of strong workplace relationships lie in trust, respect, and a shared understanding. They flourish through regular, positive interactions and a sincere concern for the welfare of others. Much like plants need consistent watering and sunlight, relationships thrive with regular attention and care.

Clear, open, and honest communication is vital for fostering robust relationships. It involves conveying your thoughts effectively, being an attentive listener, fully engaging with others, and valuing their perspectives. Successful communication is reciprocal, like traffic flowing smoothly on a two-way street.

Recognizing and appreciating the efforts and successes of others is another crucial element in relationship-building. Relationships in the workplace benefit from recognition and appreciation, just as plants in a garden do with the proper nutrition.

Moreover, being dependable and consistent is vital to building trust. When colleagues know they can rely on you, it solidifies the foundation of your relationships. It's about being steadfast, offering support and stability, much like a sturdy pillar that others can depend on.

SELF-MOTIVATION TECHNIQUES: DRIVING PERSONAL GROWTH

In Emotional Intelligence, self-motivation is akin to being your personal mentor and supporter. It's the internal force that pushes you onward, even when obstacles arise. Establishing personal targets and ambitions is a crucial element of self-motivation. Similar to a navigator setting a course, these objectives provide you with direction and intent, maintaining your focus and alignment with your broader ambitions.

However, merely setting goals isn't enough. The essence of self-motivation is found in the relentless pursuit of these objectives. This requires sustaining your enthusiasm and commitment, even when the journey is arduous. Like a long-distance runner fixed on the finish line, you must tap into your deep well of grit and perseverance.

Employing the technique of visualizing success can significantly amplify self-motivation. Picturing yourself achieving your aims and the following sense of fulfillment can act as a potent driving force, serving as a lighthouse amidst turbulent waters.

Additionally, acknowledging and celebrating each accomplishment fuels self-motivation. Recognizing even the smallest of victories can substantially boost your motivation, propelling you forward. It's like noting each landmark on an extensive expedition, each serving as a testament to the distance you've traversed and motivating you to continue.

HANDLING STRESS AND ANXIETY: EMOTIONAL RESILIENCE

Navigating stress and anxiety in our modern, fast-moving world can be likened to a sailor braving turbulent seas. Emotional resilience is akin to the skill of staying buoyant and steering through these rough waters. It's about being alert to the indicators of stress and anxiety and employing effective techniques to manage them. Much like a sturdily constructed vessel, emotional resilience equips you to endure the storm without being overwhelmed.

A vital tactic in this endeavor is mindfulness—remaining grounded in the present and consciously observing your thoughts and emotions without passing judgment. It's similar to anchoring oneself firmly in the present, preventing the currents of anxiety from dragging you away. Mindfulness techniques such as meditation and deep breathing are critical tools for fostering this sense of presence and mitigating stress.

However, resilience also leans heavily on having a supportive network. Access to people for guidance, support, or simply an empathetic ear can make a substantial difference. It's comparable to having a dedicated crew on your ship, where each member offers support and assistance throughout the voyage.

Additionally, altering your perception of stress can be advantageous. Rather than seeing it as a menace, it can be viewed as a hurdle to surmount or an opportunity for personal growth. This alteration in viewpoint can significantly change how you experience and manage stress.

DEVELOPING EMOTIONAL INSIGHT: REFLECTIVE PRACTICES

Cultivating emotional insight is akin to setting off on a profound journey towards self-exploration. It's about probing into the depths of your emotions, discerning their roots, and recognizing how they influence your actions and choices. Reflective practices like journaling or deep introspection are invaluable tools on this voyage. They act as mirrors, offering a clear view of your internal emotional landscape, enabling you to deepen your understanding of yourself.

Yet, this exploration goes beyond mere self-awareness; it's equally about self-enhancement. It involves pinpointing recurring emotional patterns and actively working to modify those that are counterproductive or harmful. Like a sculptor meticulously refining a piece of marble, this process gradually shapes your emotional reactions to align more closely with your desired self.

Incorporating feedback from others can also shed light on aspects of your emotional self that might be obscure to you. Sometimes, others can perceive facets of our emotional makeup that we overlook. Like a lighthouse revealing unseen hazards in the ocean, input from trusted peers or friends can aid in crafting a more comprehensive view of your emotional being.

Moreover, the development of emotional insight is a continuous endeavor. It demands ongoing commitment and effort. As you evolve and mature, so too will your emotional understanding, leading to enhanced emotional intelligence and greater effectiveness in your leadership role.

CONFLICT RESOLUTION AND NEGOTIATION

IDENTIFYING SOURCES OF CONFLICT: ROOT CAUSE ANALYSIS

I dentifying the sources of conflict is like a detective unraveling the threads of a mystery. It requires a keen eye for detail, an understanding of human behavior, and the patience to dig beneath the surface. Leaders must look beyond the obvious, exploring underlying issues like misaligned goals, miscommunication, or resource competition. This deep dive is crucial, as an accurate diagnosis is the first step toward effective resolution, much like a doctor identifying the root cause of an ailment before prescribing treatment.

Conflicts in the workplace can arise from multiple sources, akin to a complex piece of machinery experiencing glitches from different components. Just as a mechanic understands that problems could stem from the engine, electrical system, or transmission, a manager must recognize that workplace conflicts can originate from interpersonal dynamics, organizational structures, or even external pressures. This awareness is crucial, much like a skilled mechanic's ability to diagnose issues based on the part of the machinery affected, ensuring that the appropriate solution is applied to each unique problem.

Active listening plays a crucial role in identifying sources of conflict. Leaders can gather the necessary insights to understand the conflict's roots by listening attentively to all parties involved. This process is like an archaeologist carefully excavating a site, uncovering layer after layer to reveal the artifacts beneath.

Leaders must also be aware of their biases and assumptions, which can cloud judgment and hinder the accurate identification of conflict sources. Regular self-reflection and seeking external perspectives can help mitigate this, like cleaning a window to get a clearer view outside.

Finally, documenting and analyzing past conflicts can provide valuable insights into common sources and patterns. This historical perspective can help leaders anticipate and address potential conflicts before they escalate, like a meteorologist studying past weather patterns to predict future conditions.

NEGOTIATION STRATEGIES: FINDING WIN-WIN SOLUTIONS

Negotiation is a nuanced art form that demands a delicate balance of assertiveness, empathy, and strategic thinking with adaptability. The aim is to achieve outcomes where all parties feel their needs are acknowledged and fulfilled. This process is comparable to that of a choreographer, who skillfully blends the unique talents of individual dancers to produce a harmonious and unified performance.

In negotiation, thorough preparation is crucial. Gaining a comprehensive understanding of all parties' needs, interests, and limitations paves the way for more effective and strategic dialogue. This is similar to a military general analyzing the battlefield to formulate a well-thought-out strategy.

Skilled negotiators employ various tactics tailored to each specific situation. Approaches like principled negotiation, which concentrates on shared interests rather than rigid positions, often result in more cooperative and enduring agreements. It's analogous to two architects collaboratively designing a structure that encapsulates the vision of both.

Emotional intelligence in negotiations is akin to a seasoned chef perfectly adjusting the flavors in a dish. Just as the chef uses their senses to gauge the balance of ingredients and subtly alter them to achieve the desired taste, a negotiator with high emotional intelligence reads the room, understands the undercurrents of emotions, and adjusts their approach accordingly. This skill allows them to steer the negotiation favorably, like a chef expertly bringing a dish to its peak flavor.

Lastly, adopting a long-term outlook is vital in negotiation. The objective is not merely to triumph in the immediate scenario but to cultivate relationships that pave the way for positive future interactions. It's similar to planting a tree: the most significant rewards are harvested over time, extending far beyond the initial planting.

MEDIATING TEAM DISPUTES: NEUTRAL FACILITATION

Acting as a mediator in team disputes calls for an impartial and objective approach, akin to a referee overseeing a sports match. The mediator's duty is to foster a dialogue where all parties can voice their opinions and collaboratively seek a solution. This role involves establishing clear guidelines to ensure balanced and respectful exchanges and steering conversations toward productive ends.

Creating a space of trust and confidentiality is essential for mediators. It's crucial for team members to feel comfortable sharing their thoughts and emotions without fear of negative consequences. This sense of security is the bedrock of effective mediation, much like a strong foundation is essential for a sturdy house.

For mediators, active listening and empathy are indispensable skills. By fully understanding each individual's point of view and emotional state, it becomes possible to unearth mutual understanding and viable solutions. This is similar to the role of a translator, who interprets the words and captures the underlying emotions and intentions.

Additionally, mediators need proficiency in conflict resolution strategies, such as highlighting key points, reinterpreting issues, and considering alternative approaches. These methods are pivotal in maintaining focused and constructive dialogue, like a guide navigating travelers through intricate and challenging routes.

Post-mediation follow-up is also crucial. Ensuring the implementation of agreed-upon actions and keeping an eye on the long-term effectiveness of the resolution can stave off future conflicts.

PREVENTIVE MEASURES FOR CONFLICT: PROACTIVE STRATEGIES

Preventing conflict is often more effective than resolving it after the fact. Proactive strategies involve creating a team environment where the potential for conflict is minimized. This can include setting clear expectations, fostering open communication, and building strong relationships among team members. It's like weatherproofing a house to protect it from storms.

Encouraging regular team-building activities can strengthen relationships and improve understanding among team members. These activities can range from professional development workshops to informal social events. Like shared experiences that bond people, these activities create a stronger, more cohesive team.

Leaders should also model the behavior they wish to see in their team. Demonstrating effective communication, respecting diverse opinions, and managing stress in healthy ways sets a standard for the team to follow. It's similar to a parent setting an example for their children.

Establishing a clear process for addressing issues and concerns can also prevent conflicts. When team members know how and where to express their concerns, issues can be addressed before they escalate into larger conflicts. It's like having a clear and accessible emergency exit in a building. Finally, regularly reviewing team processes, dynamics, and workloads can help identify potential sources of conflict early on.

HANDLING PERSONAL CONFLICT: MAINTAINING PROFESSIONALISM

Handling personal conflict in a professional setting requires a delicate balance between addressing the issue and maintaining a professional demeanor. The first step is to acknowledge the conflict and the emotions involved, much like a doctor acknowledges a patient's pain before treating it.

Maintaining professionalism means focusing on the issue at hand and not letting personal emotions dictate your actions. It involves clear, calm communication and a willingness to understand the other person's perspective. Much like a diplomat navigating sensitive negotiations, the goal is to resolve the issue while maintaining respect and decorum.

Seeking a resolution that satisfies all parties involved is the ideal outcome. This might involve compromise, collaboration, or seeking external mediation. It's like finding the perfect recipe that suits everyone's tastes.

Setting boundaries is also important. This means knowing what behavior is acceptable and what isn't and being prepared to enforce these boundaries respectfully and firmly. It's akin to setting rules of engagement in a debate, ensuring the discussion remains constructive and respectful.

Lastly, reflecting on personal conflicts and learning from them can provide valuable insights for future interactions. Understanding what triggered the conflict, how it was handled, and how it could be prevented in the future is crucial for personal and professional development, much like an athlete reviewing game footage to improve their performance.

BUILDING A CULTURE OF COLLABORATION: ENCOURAGING TEAMWORK

Cultivating a collaborative culture is akin to growing a communal garden where each individual's input leads to collective prosperity. It's about creating a space where the spirit of teamwork is not just appreciated but actively cultivated and rewarded. Leaders are instrumental in this process, setting the precedent and exemplifying teamwork in their actions.

Promoting open dialogue and idea-sharing is essential for fostering collaboration. When team members feel that their contributions are acknowledged and valued, they're more inclined to engage actively. This environment, where ideas freely flow and merge, resembles a dynamic brainstorming session where the most effective solutions are born from joint efforts.

Offering chances for team members to collaborate on projects, address challenges, or spearhead new initiatives is a great way to bolster collaborative abilities. Similar to how players on a sports team learn to synergize their skills to achieve victory, colleagues learn to harness each other's strengths and balance out their weaknesses.

Acknowledging and celebrating collective achievements plays a key role in underscoring the importance of teamwork. Recognition, whether through formal programs or casual commendation, for achievements born from teamwork is as vital as giving a round of applause to a choir after a captivating performance.

Finally, investing in training and resources to hone collaborative skills can significantly improve a team's cooperative effectiveness. Providing workshops focused on teamwork, communication, or problem-solving is akin to outfitting a group of hikers with all the necessary equipment and guidance for a successful trek.

LEARNING FROM CONFLICT: GROWTH OPPORTUNITIES

Viewing conflict as an opportunity for growth is like seeing challenges as stepping stones to improvement. It involves a mindset shift from avoiding conflict to embracing it as a chance to learn, develop, and strengthen relationships. This perspective can transform potentially negative experiences into valuable lessons.

Reflecting on conflicts after they have been resolved can provide insights into personal and team dynamics. Understanding what led to the conflict, how it was handled, and the outcomes can inform future interactions and decision-making, much like a scientist analyzing the results of an experiment to gain a deeper understanding.

Leaders can use conflicts as teaching moments for their teams. Discussing conflicts openly and constructively can help team members learn from these experiences and develop better conflict-resolution skills. It's like a coach using game footage to teach players how to improve their strategy and technique.

Encouraging a culture where feedback and constructive criticism are part of the learning process can also stem from conflict resolution. It's about creating an environment where learning from mistakes is valued, much like in an academic setting where critical analysis and debate are encouraged.

Finally, applying the lessons learned from conflicts to make positive changes can lead to continuous improvement in both personal and team performance. It's about turning challenges into catalysts for growth, much like an artist who uses criticism to refine and evolve their work.

LEADING HIGH-PERFORMANCE TEAMS

SETTING CLEAR GOALS AND OBJECTIVES: VISION ALIGNMENT

Coordinating a high-performance team around well-defined goals is like meticulously charting a course on a maritime map. Each team member must be clear about the destination and their specific role in reaching it. Setting distinct, measurable, and achievable objectives acts as a guiding light, akin to a lighthouse illuminating the path for ships at night. Such clarity ensures that efforts are harmonized, with every member contributing effectively towards the common goal.

Involving the team in setting these goals can make these targets more impactful and attainable. It's about fostering a sense of shared responsibility and dedication, much like a ship's crew participating in charting their collective course. This inclusive method empowers the team and taps into their collective intelligence and creativity.

Flexibility in adjusting goals and objectives is crucial, mirroring how a vessel must adapt its sails to shifting winds. Leaders should be prepared to modify objectives in light of new challenges, market shifts, or changes within the team. This adaptability ensures that the team remains nimble and equipped to steer through any circumstance to meet their goals.

Moreover, celebrating the milestones and progress towards these objectives is vital. Recognizing accomplishments along the way bolsters morale and drives motivation for the remaining journey. It's comparable to noting significant points during an extensive voyage, acknowledging both the distance traversed and the path that lies ahead.

FOSTERING TEAM COLLABORATION: ENHANCING COOPERATION

Fostering collaboration in a team is like cultivating a rich, biodiverse ecosystem. Each member contributes unique skills and perspectives, and their cooperative interactions lead to the team's success. Cultivating a space where open dialogue, mutual regard, and common objectives flourish is akin to the artistry of a chef in the kitchen. Imagine a culinary maestro meticulously selecting and combining unique ingredients. Each spice, herb, or vegetable brings its own essence, yet when melded together, they form a symphony of flavors that is more delightful and complex than any single component. This harmony in the dish is the chef's signature, a testament to their skill in balancing diverse flavors. Similarly, a leader carefully blends a team's varied talents and viewpoints, crafting an environment where every individual contribution enhances the collective outcome, creating a workplace that's as rich and satisfying as a well-prepared meal.

Regular team interactions and open dialogue are foundational for enhancing cooperation. Structured meetings, brainstorming sessions, and informal gatherings create opportunities for team members to connect, share ideas, and build relationships. This ongoing interaction is like watering a garden, which is essential for maintaining its health and vitality.

Conflict management is an integral part of fostering team collaboration. Effectively navigating disagreements can strengthen team dynamics. Addressing conflicts with empathy and focusing on shared goals can transform potential roadblocks into opportunities for growth and deeper understanding, much like a blacksmith forges a stronger blade through fire and hammering.

Incorporating team-building activities can also strengthen the bonds of collaboration. These work-related or social activities allow team members to understand each other's strengths and weaknesses, fostering a sense of unity and teamwork. Like the intertwined roots of plants in a garden, these shared experiences create a strong foundation for effective collaboration.

PERFORMANCE MANAGEMENT: EVALUATING TEAM PROGRESS

Effective performance management in a high-performance team is akin to a navigator constantly adjusting the ship's course. Regular assessments of the team's progress toward their goals, constructive feedback, and necessary adjustments ensure that the team stays on the right path. This ongoing evaluation is about measuring outcomes and understanding the processes and behaviors that drive those results.

Continuous feedback is an essential component of this process. Rather than limiting feedback to periodic reviews, it involves regular, constructive interactions that guide team members toward improved performance. This approach is like a coach providing real-time guidance to athletes, helping them refine their field techniques.

Adapting strategies based on performance feedback is vital. Leaders should be ready to alter tactics or approaches in response to the team's performance, ensuring the team's continual advancement towards its goals. This adaptability is like a plant bending towards the sunlight, constantly adjusting itself to grow optimally.

Recognizing individual contributions while evaluating team performance is also essential. Acknowledging each member's role in the team's success fosters a sense of belonging and appreciation. It's like a conductor highlighting the soloists while appreciating the entire orchestra's harmony.

CULTIVATING TEAM TALENT: ENCOURAGING DEVELOPMENT

Nurturing the talents of a team in a high-performance setting can be likened to tending a diverse and flourishing garden. Each team member possesses distinct abilities and potential that, when adequately cultivated, can significantly enhance the team's collective success. This nurturing process involves identifying individual strengths and providing avenues for growth, including training, mentorship, and stimulating projects. Much like a knowledgeable gardener who knows precisely what each plant needs to flourish, a leader must discern and fulfill each team member's specific developmental requirements.

Establishing ongoing learning and development opportunities is fundamental. Motivating team members to acquire new knowledge and skills keeps the team vibrant, forward-thinking, and prepared to tackle novel challenges. It's akin to enriching the soil of a garden, fortifying the team's base with innovative ideas and fresh perspectives.

Creating an atmosphere where every team member feels empowered to grow and apply their talents fully is essential. This means offering the necessary tools, support, and independence to explore and expand. Similar to how sunlight is vital for plants' photosynthesis and growth, a supportive and liberating environment is key to fostering team members' advancement and capability.

Moreover, encouraging collaborative efforts across different functions can further elevate team talent. Engaging with colleagues from various departments allows individuals to gain new insights, broaden their skill sets, and appreciate a variety of viewpoints. This exchange of abilities and knowledge resembles the mutual benefits that different plant species derive from one another in a vibrant ecosystem.

CREATING AN INCLUSIVE ENVIRONMENT: VALUING DIVERSITY

Fostering an inclusive atmosphere in a high-performance team is similar to crafting a richly varied painting. Every team member contributes distinct hues to the artwork, enhancing the overall aesthetic. Embracing inclusivity means recognizing and cherishing this diversity and understanding that the varied backgrounds, experiences, and viewpoints of each individual augment the team's richness. Like a colorful mosaic, the team derives its strength and vibrancy from its diverse elements.

However, promoting inclusivity goes beyond merely recognizing diversity; it entails proactive measures to ensure every team member feels valued and understood. This could involve enacting diversity-supportive policies, offering inclusivity training, and cultivating an environment where varied opinions are acknowledged and esteemed. Like a symphony where different instruments harmonize, the team should unify its diverse members into a coherent and effective ensemble.

Providing equal opportunities for everyone's participation and growth is essential. True inclusivity isn't just about the presence of diversity; it's about empowering every member to contribute significantly and develop. Giving each member their moment to shine, akin to spotlighting every musician in an orchestra, allows for the recognition and appreciation of individual skills.

Celebrating this diversity regularly can further enrich an inclusive environment. Recognizing cultural events, encouraging open dialogues about diversity, and celebrating each team member's unique contributions underscore inclusivity's importance. This celebration is like a garden where every flower, irrespective of its origin, is cherished and admired for its distinct beauty.

EMPOWERING TEAM AUTONOMY: TRUST AND RESPONSIBILITY

Empowering team autonomy in a high-performance setting is like a teacher giving students the freedom to lead their own projects. It involves trusting team members to make decisions, take initiative, and lead in their areas of expertise. This empowerment boosts morale and encourages a sense of ownership and responsibility, like allowing young learners to steer their learning journey, which instills confidence and independence.

Granting autonomy requires a balance between freedom and guidance. It's about providing enough space for team members to innovate and problem-solve independently while remaining available to offer support and direction. This balance is like that of a gardener, who allows plants to grow on their own but prunes them when necessary to encourage healthy growth.

Regular check-ins and support are essential to empowering autonomy. Leaders must ensure that, while autonomy is encouraged, team members do not feel abandoned. This approach ensures that the team feels supported in their autonomous roles while maintaining alignment with its overall objectives. It's like a safety net for a trapeze artist, providing security while allowing for an exhilarating performance.

Encouraging a culture where mistakes are viewed as learning opportunities can further empower team autonomy. When team members know they can take calculated risks without fear of harsh judgment, they are more likely to experiment and innovate. This culture is like a laboratory where scientists are free to explore and discover, knowing that every outcome offers valuable insights, whether expected or not.

CELEBRATING TEAM ACHIEVEMENTS: RECOGNIZING SUCCESS

Celebrating team achievements in a high-performance environment is crucial, much like the applause that follows a stunning performance. It's about acknowledging the team's hard work, commitment, and success. This recognition boosts morale and reinforces the behaviors and practices that led to those achievements. Celebrations can take various forms, from formal award ceremonies to casual team gatherings, but the essence is to create moments of shared joy and appreciation.

Regular recognition of both big and small victories is important. Celebrating significant milestones is as necessary as acknowledging the smaller steps that lead to those milestones. This ongoing recognition is like cheering for a runner at various points along the race, not just at the finish line.

Integrating recognition into the team's culture strengthens the sense of unity and appreciation. Whether through shout-outs in meetings, thank-you notes, or reward systems, consistent recognition nurtures a positive team environment. It's like watering a plant regularly, ensuring its steady growth and blooming.

Tailoring celebrations to suit the team's culture and preferences can make them more meaningful. Understanding what types of recognition resonate with the team ensures that the celebrations are genuinely appreciated. It's like a chef who knows their diners' tastes and customizes the meal to delight them.

Recognizing individual contributions to the team's successes is also essential. While celebrating team achievements, highlighting individual efforts and talents can foster a sense of personal accomplishment and belonging. It's like a mosaic, where each unique piece contributes to the overall beauty of the artwork.

Encouraging team members to celebrate each other's successes builds a supportive and collaborative culture. When team members appreciate and acknowledge each other's achievements, it creates a positive feedback loop of recognition and motivation. This environment is like a society of mutual admiration, where each member uplifts and inspires the others.

Lastly, reflecting on the journey to these achievements is as important as the celebration itself. It allows the team to reflect on the challenges overcome, lessons learned, and growth experienced. This reflection is like pausing at the summit of a mountain to look back at the path traveled, appreciating the journey as much as the destination.

DECISION MAKING AND PROBLEM SOLVING

ANALYTICAL THINKING: BREAKING DOWN COMPLEXITIES

Decision-making that incorporates analytical thinking is similar to a skilled mechanic meticulously dismantling a complex engine. Each aspect of the problem is scrutinized, thoroughly understood, and evaluated for its role in the larger issue. This detailed approach fosters a profound comprehension of the problem, ensuring solutions target the root causes rather than merely addressing superficial symptoms. Like a detective methodically assembling clues to unravel a mystery, a leader employs analytical thinking to reveal the true essence of a challenge.

In this endeavor, utilizing a range of analytical methods is essential. Techniques like creating flowcharts, conducting root cause analyses, or holding brainstorming sessions offer diverse viewpoints, each shedding light on different facets of

43

the issue. It's akin to examining an object through various lenses, with each one presenting a fresh perspective.

Moreover, nurturing an environment that encourages team members to actively participate in analytical thinking enhances problem-solving. When individuals with varied backgrounds and skills apply their analytical talents, the result is a deeper and more holistic understanding of complex issues. This collective analysis is comparable to a group of musicians, each contributing their unique style to a collaborative jam session, resulting in a richer and more intricate composition.

Additionally, incorporating technology into analytical thinking can greatly boost its impact. Modern tools and software offer advanced capabilities for data analysis, recognizing patterns, and modeling scenarios. Leveraging these technological resources is like equipping a scientist with cutting-edge laboratory tools, significantly improving the efficacy and speed of their inquiries.

CREATIVE PROBLEM SOLVING: INNOVATIVE APPROACHES

Creative problem-solving in leadership is much like an artist transforming a bare canvas into a mesmerizing work of art. It necessitates transcending traditional boundaries and venturing into less explored territories to discover groundbreaking solutions. Leaders need to foster an environment where imagination flourishes, inspiring team members to brainstorm and think outside the confines of conventional methods. This freedom of creativity can spark revolutionary solutions that shift the problem-solving paradigm.

Cultivating a culture that champions innovation and creativity is crucial. This means nurturing an open-minded space where every idea is appreciated and explored regardless of how offbeat it might seem. Such an atmosphere acts as a rich soil for imagination, allowing the seeds of creativity to sprout and grow, free from the constraints of judgment or doubt.

However, marrying creativity with practicality is a delicate but necessary part of problem-solving. While encouraging avant-garde thinking is important, solutions must remain viable and actionable. It's about finding the perfect equilibrium between imaginative ideas and their pragmatic implementation, ensuring that creative solutions are not only novel but also workable.

Moreover, creative problem-solving often entails seeking inspiration from various domains and experiences. Leaders should motivate their teams to cast their nets wide for inspiration, like inventors combining elements from different fields to forge something new. This intermingling of thoughts and perspectives can culminate in unique and effective solutions.

INFORMED DECISION MAKING: DATA-DRIVEN CHOICES

In management, making informed decisions is akin to an experienced hiker navigating a complex trail with a detailed map and a reliable GPS. It involves a deep dive into data, keenly following market trends, and leaning on solid empirical evidence, much like how a hiker would use every tool at their disposal to traverse tricky terrain. This systematic approach ensures that decisions aren't mere guesses but carefully charted steps, reminiscent of a seasoned explorer who combines their savvy with state-of-the-art equipment for the best outcomes. Just as a scientist meticulously draws conclusions from thorough research and experiments, a savvy manager sifts through data and insights, ensuring every decision is as informed and precise as possible.

Utilizing sophisticated data analytics tools can significantly improve the decision-making process. These tools act like advanced telescopes, bringing far-off and unclear data into sharp focus, enabling leaders to make choices grounded in extensive and detailed insights. They assist in navigating through the vast sea of data to pinpoint the precise information necessary for well-informed decisions.

However, it's crucial to blend this data-driven approach with human insight. Leaders should interpret data through the lens of their industry expertise and their organization's unique culture. It involves deciphering the narratives the numbers tell, akin to a historian who makes sense of the past through artifacts. This human element ensures that decisions are not only rational but also pertinent and considerate of the individuals involved.

Furthermore, fostering an environment where data is routinely gathered, analyzed, and leveraged can revolutionize an organization. When team members recognize the significance of data in shaping decisions, they're more inclined to contribute to and embrace a data-oriented strategy. This atmosphere, reminiscent of a scientific community that bases theories and methods on data and evidence, promotes a culture of informed and efficient decision-making across the organization.

RISK ASSESSMENT AND MANAGEMENT:
NAVIGATING UNCERTAINTIES

Risk assessment and management in decision-making are as crucial as a ship's captain rigorously planning for various maritime conditions before setting out. This involves identifying possible risks, evaluating their impact, and devising strategies to mitigate them, like an architect designs a building to withstand different environmental challenges, ensuring its long-term resilience and stability.

Developing a detailed risk management plan is vital. This plan serves as a safeguard, similar to a safety net for a trapeze artist, offering a structured method for spotting and addressing potential risks. It requires continual reassessment and updating risk strategies to keep them pertinent and effective in a dynamic environment.

Promoting a mindset of risk awareness within the organization is fundamental. When team members are vigilant about potential risks and understand their role in mitigating them, the entire organization becomes sturdier. This shared vigilance is like a community collectively bracing for natural disasters, where each individual's preparedness fortifies the community's overall security and resilience.

Integrating risk management into all significant decision-making processes is also imperative. Leaders should consider potential risks in every crucial decision, akin to a surgeon contemplating potential complications before a procedure. This approach ensures that decisions are not only strategic but also prudent, taking into consideration potential difficulties and uncertainties.

Furthermore, employing technology in risk assessment can provide more profound insights and accurate predictions. Contemporary tools can sift through vast amounts of data to identify trends and hidden risks. Utilizing these advanced technologies is similar to providing a meteorologist with state-of-the-art tools for more accurately forecasting weather, enhancing their capacity to prepare for and efficiently manage risks.

COLLECTIVE DECISION MAKING: LEVERAGING TEAM INPUT

Group decision-making taps into the collective intelligence and varied perspectives of the team, much like how each actor in an ensemble cast adds depth to the overall performance. It encompasses weaving together team members' different insights and viewpoints into the decision-making fabric. This method yields more comprehensive decisions and cultivates a sense of participation and dedication among the team.

Creating an environment that promotes open discussions and uninhibited idea-sharing is vital for successful group decision-making. In this setting, akin to a roundtable, everyone should have the chance to express their thoughts and influence the ultimate decision. This inclusive approach guarantees that various experiences and viewpoints enhance decisions, resulting in more fair and informed outcomes.

Maintaining a balance between this collaborative process and decisive leadership is essential. While the input from the team is critical, the leader must steer the conversation toward a definitive resolution.

It's also important to be aware of and manage the dynamics inherent in group decision-making. Leaders should be alert to tendencies like groupthink, where a preference for agreement might overshadow diverse opinions. Cultivating a space where different viewpoints are tolerated and actively encouraged is crucial. This environment, comparable to a biodiverse ecosystem, flourishes from the diversity and richness it embraces, leading to healthier and stronger decision-making.

Moreover, integrating technology can amplify group decision-making. Digital tools and platforms can streamline idea sharing and collaboration, particularly in geographically dispersed teams. They also promote more democratic and transparent decision-making. Employing these technologies is like arming the team with advanced communication tools, ensuring every perspective is acknowledged and valued, regardless of location.

OVERCOMING DECISION PARALYSIS: CONFIDENCE IN CHOICES

Confronting decision paralysis is comparable to a mountaineer facing the daunting challenge of a difficult ascent. It necessitates the bravery to evaluate choices and make decisions, even under uncertain circumstances. Often, decision paralysis arises from the apprehension of making incorrect choices. However, just as a climber must decide on a route to the summit, a leader must make choices to drive the team forward.

Cultivating confidence in decision-making is a gradual process. Leaders develop this assurance by reflecting on their previous decisions and drawing lessons from both triumphs and setbacks. Similar to an athlete analyzing past game footage, this introspection aids in enhancing future performance and accumulating a wealth of experiences to inform new decisions.

Establishing a culture that embraces calculated risk-taking and perceives errors as learning moments can help alleviate decision paralysis. Such an environment, akin to a practice field, allows team members to make decisions without excessive fear of negative consequences, nurturing an active and enterprising team ethos.

Additionally, providing the team with structured decision-making frameworks and tools can clarify and simplify the process. These resources serve as navigational aids, assisting in traversing intricate scenarios and systematically evaluating various options, much like a navigator's tools offer vital information and perspective for informed decision-making.

Moreover, creating a supportive atmosphere where team members feel their input and decisions are valued can enhance confidence in making decisions. Leaders should foster a space where team members are reassured that they have their leaders' support, similar to how a safety harness secures a climber. This backing encourages individuals to take the initiative and make decisions with more assurance.

LEARNING FROM MISTAKES: CONSTRUCTIVE REFLECTIONS

Adopting a learning mindset towards mistakes in decision-making is a critical component of ongoing improvement and growth. This approach involves viewing errors not as failures but as valuable lessons for personal and professional development. Each misstep offers insights that can enhance future decisions, similar to how a scientist gains valuable knowledge from every experiment, regardless of its outcome.

Reflecting on mistakes ought to be a systematic and constructive exercise, concentrating on dissecting what went wrong, its causes, and ways to prevent similar occurrences in the future. This process, akin to a team reviewing a project's outcomes, is instrumental in pinpointing key learnings and strategies for improvement. The focus isn't on pointing fingers but on learning together from the experience.

Cultivating a team environment where errors are openly discussed and used as learning tools can create a safer, more innovative space. When team members understand that they can take calculated risks and that their mistakes will be viewed as learning moments, they're more inclined to suggest innovative ideas and take bold actions. This environment resembles a research lab, where experiments are conducted for the sake of learning and discovery, not just for success.

Implementing feedback and learning structures is also crucial. After-action reviews or consistent feedback sessions can systematically extract the lessons from errors. These systems function like reflective tools, showcasing the team's performance and highlighting both their strong points and areas needing improvement.

Moreover, leaders need to model this learning approach. By transparently sharing their own errors and the subsequent learnings, leaders establish a precedent that mistakes are a natural and essential part of the learning journey. This transparency, akin to a teacher sharing experiences with students, can encourage team members to approach their own learning paths with more openness and less apprehension.

MOTIVATING AND INSPIRING
YOUR TEAM

UNDERSTANDING MOTIVATION: DIFFERENT
MOTIVATORS

U nderstanding what drives each team member is like a botanist recognizing the unique conditions each plant needs to thrive. Everyone has their own motivators, influenced by personal values, experiences, and goals. Leaders must act like skilled gardeners, identifying and nurturing these individual motivators to cultivate a motivated and thriving team. This personalized approach ensures each team member's potential is fully realized, like providing the right soil and sunlight for different plants.

Recognizing that motivators can change over time is also crucial. Just as a plant's needs may vary from seedling to full bloom, so too can an individual's drivers. Regular check-ins and open communication help leaders stay attuned to these evolving needs, allowing them to adjust motivational strategies accordingly. It's a dynamic process requiring ongoing attention and adaptation.

Additionally, understanding motivation involves acknowledging the intrinsic and extrinsic factors that drive individuals. Some people may find their drive from outside rewards and recognition, while others find it from within, seeking personal development or alignment with their values. Leaders must cater to this spectrum of motivators, crafting a motivational strategy as diverse as the team itself.

Furthermore, mapping the motivation of the team can provide valuable insights. This involves identifying individual motivators and understanding how these drivers interact within the team dynamic. It's about creating a holistic strategy that recognizes the complex web of motivations at play, ensuring that the approach to motivation is as nuanced and multifaceted as the team itself.

SETTING INSPIRATIONAL GOALS: ASPIRATIONAL OBJECTIVES

Setting inspirational goals is about charting a course that directs and uplifts the team. These goals should spark ambition and ignite a passion for achievement. They need to resonate on a deeper level, connecting with the team's aspirations and driving them to stretch beyond their perceived limits. Like a beacon on a hill, these goals guide and inspire, pulling the team forward through both inspiration and aspiration.

Crafting these goals requires a blend of ambition and realism. They should be challenging enough to inspire and attainable enough to maintain motivation. It's about striking a balance, much like an architect designs a building that is both aesthetically awe-inspiring and structurally sound. Leaders must ensure that these aspirational objectives are grounded in reality, providing a clear path to achievement.

Moreover, involving the team in goal-setting can significantly enhance their motivational power. When team members contribute to shaping the goals, they're more likely to feel a strong personal connection to them. This collaborative approach is like a choir composing a song together; each voice adds a unique layer, creating a piece that resonates with all.

In addition, setting various short-term and long-term goals can keep motivation consistent and evolving. While long-term goals provide a grand vision to strive towards, short-term goals offer immediate challenges and victories, keeping the team engaged and motivated. It's a layered approach, ensuring there's always something to inspire and drive the team forward.

CREATING A POSITIVE WORK ENVIRONMENT: CULTURE OF ENTHUSIASM

A constructive work atmosphere is the fertile soil from which motivation and inspiration sprout. It's centered on fostering a culture imbued with enthusiasm, respect, and support as its cornerstones. In such an environment, team members feel more appreciated and energized, similar to how plants flourish in a carefully tended garden. Leaders must cultivate and maintain this environment, ensuring it's always a thriving space conducive to growth.

In this culture, positivity is more than just encouraged; it's woven into the very fabric of every interaction, policy, and decision. It involves creating an ecosystem where positive energy flourishes, influencing everything from the celebration of successes to the approach to overcoming challenges. Like a vibrant habitat that nurtures diverse species, a positive work environment nurtures a varied team, enabling each individual to prosper.

Moreover, this culture of positivity must be consistent and genuine. It should represent a deeply ingrained part of the organizational identity, not just a superficial veneer that fades in adversity. This genuineness is akin to the deep roots of a sturdy tree, offering steadfast support and sustenance regardless of the changing weather.

Promoting open dialogue and a sense of community can also significantly enhance this positive setting. When team members feel free to express themselves and have a sense of belonging to a caring collective, their motivation and contentment naturally elevate. It's like fostering a space where everyone communicates in a mutual language of respect and support, cultivating a sense of unity and collective mission.

RECOGNITION AND REWARDS: VALUING CONTRIBUTIONS

Recognition and rewards are powerful tools in a leader's motivational arsenal. They're about acknowledging team members' hard work and achievements and validating their efforts and contributions. This recognition goes beyond mere acknowledgment; it's a statement of value, showing team members that what they do matters and is appreciated.

Like applause at the end of a performance, it boosts morale and encourages continued excellence.

Tailoring these rewards and recognitions to individual preferences can greatly enhance their impact. Some may appreciate public accolades, while others might prefer private recognition or tangible rewards. Understanding and catering to these individual preferences is like a chef preparing a meal tailored to each diner's taste, ensuring the experience is enjoyable and memorable.

Additionally, ensuring that recognition is timely and relevant is essential. Acknowledging achievements as they happen makes the recognition more impactful and meaningful. It's akin to watering a plant at the right time; timely nourishment enhances growth and vitality.

Furthermore, integrating recognition into the team's regular rhythm can help maintain a constant level of motivation. It shouldn't be an afterthought or a rare occurrence but a regular part of the team's operations. Regular recognition is like a steady rain that nourishes the soil, consistently supporting growth and development.

PERSONAL DEVELOPMENT OPPORTUNITIES: GROWTH PATHS

Offering personal development opportunities is similar to providing a map and compass to explorers eager to discover new territories. It's about giving team members the tools and resources to navigate their own growth paths, aligning their personal and professional development with the organization's goals. By investing in their growth, leaders motivate their team members and build a more skilled and capable team.

Providing various development opportunities caters to a team's diverse needs and aspirations. From training and workshops to mentoring and challenging projects, each type of opportunity offers a different path for growth. It's like providing different genres of books to a group of avid readers, each catering to different interests and styles.

Encouraging self-directed learning and development fosters a sense of autonomy and self-efficacy. When team members are empowered to take charge of their growth, they're more engaged and motivated. It's akin to teaching someone to fish rather than just giving them a fish, providing skills and confidence that last a lifetime.

In addition, creating clear pathways for career advancement within the organization can significantly boost motivation. When team members see opportunities for growth and advancement, they are more likely to be committed and motivated. It's like showing climbers not just the path to the summit but also the various camps they can reach along the way, each offering its own rewards and views.

LEADING BY EXAMPLE: INSPIRATIONAL LEADERSHIP

Setting an example as a leader is arguably one of the most impactful ways to inspire others. It involves living out the behaviors and values that you want to see in your team. Leaders who exemplify commitment, optimism, and resilience establish a benchmark for others to follow. This kind of leadership transcends mere instruction; it's about demonstrating, through action, the path to excellence.

An inspiring leader is not just a figurehead but an active participant, sharing both the burdens and triumphs with the team. They don't simply assign tasks; they're actively engaged, working shoulder-to-shoulder with their team members. Such hands-on involvement signifies a level of commitment and dedication that can profoundly motivate and rally the team.

Being transparent and honest as a leader also builds trust and garners respect. When leaders are candid about their challenges, decisions, and reasons, it cultivates a climate of transparency and comprehension. It's comparable to a guide sharing the entire map and the chosen path with their group, ensuring everyone is well-informed and united in the shared journey.

Additionally, displaying vulnerability and humility can be extraordinarily inspirational. Leaders who admit their errors and are willing to learn and evolve from these experiences set a powerful precedent. It underscores the aim of not faultlessness but growth, education, and ongoing betterment. This approach, akin to an experienced teacher who continues to embrace learning, encourages a culture of modesty and continuous personal development.

BUILDING TEAM SPIRIT: UNITY AND MORALE BOOSTING

Nurturing team spirit involves creating a sense of unity and camaraderie beyond professional ties. It's about cultivating a connection that resembles a family more than a mere assembly of coworkers. Engaging in activities that promote bonding, shared experiences, and a feeling of inclusivity plays a crucial role in forging robust team spirit. Much like the roots of a tree intertwining to provide mutual support, a cohesive team stands resiliently together.

Promoting open communication and collaboration is key to reinforcing this spirit. As team members collaboratively strive towards shared objectives, surmount obstacles, and revel in their successes, they forge a stronger connection. This collaboration is similar to an orchestra, where each musician's part enriches the whole, creating a harmonious and unified performance.

Facilitating chances for the team to mingle in casual environments can also elevate morale and foster unity. Social gatherings, team excursions, or relaxed meet-ups offer opportunities for team members to relate on a personal level, solidifying their professional relationships. This is like neighbors participating in a community event, where communal activities strengthen the bonds of fellowship and belonging.

Moreover, celebrating the diversity within the team can significantly boost team spirit. Appreciating and valuing the distinctive backgrounds, experiences, and viewpoints each individual contributes leads to a more inclusive and bonded team. This approach is like a tapestry that derives its beauty from a variety of threads, with each distinct thread contributing its own unique color and texture to the complete picture.

LEVERAGING TECHNOLOGY FOR EFFICIENCY

TECHNOLOGICAL TOOLS FOR MANAGERS: SOFTWARE AND APPS

In contemporary management, technological tools function as multipurpose assets for leaders, like Swiss Army knives, offering versatile solutions for various challenges. Management-oriented software and applications can greatly streamline operations, improve communication, and aid in making informed decisions. These tools are comparable to a navigator's various instruments, each fulfilling a distinct role—be it tracking progress, organizing schedules, or managing budgets—and ultimately steering the team towards its objectives more efficiently.

Identifying and embracing suitable technological tools can revolutionize a manager's approach. It involves selecting software and apps that align with the team's specific requirements and tasks. This process is much like a chef handpicking the perfect ingredients for a recipe; the choice of ingredients significantly elevates the quality of the dish.

However, navigating through the plethora of technological options demands careful consideration. Managers need to thoughtfully evaluate available tools, like how a librarian selectively curates books for a library, ensuring that each chosen tool brings value and corresponds with the team's needs and goals.

Furthermore, adequate training and familiarization with these technologies are essential. Devoting time to thoroughly understand and exploit these tools' capabilities is similar to a musician dedicating themselves to mastering an instrument, which results in a more synchronized and effective performance.

DIGITAL COMMUNICATION CHANNELS: EFFECTIVE ONLINE INTERACTION

Digital communication platforms have fundamentally transformed team interactions, eliminating physical boundaries and enabling instant connections. These channels act as virtual bridges, linking team members whether they are just across the hall or across the globe. Utilizing these platforms effectively ensures a seamless flow of ideas, feedback, and updates, akin to a well-designed roadway network enabling smooth and rapid travel.

Selecting the most suitable communication tools is critical. Depending on their specific requirements, different teams might need various tools for real-time collaboration, file sharing, or managing projects. This choice is similar to a conductor selecting the appropriate instruments for a symphony, each contributing to the overall harmony of the piece.

Observing proper digital communication etiquette is equally important. Just as social norms govern in-person interactions, online communication also follows certain best practices to ensure clarity, respectfulness, and efficiency. Adhering to these guidelines is like respecting traffic rules ensuring a safe and efficient experience for all participants.

Training in digital communication tools and understanding proper online etiquette are also crucial. Similar to training for operating new equipment, team members need to be proficient in using these digital platforms. Such training ensures that the team fully capitalizes on the capabilities of these tools, thereby boosting collaboration and productivity.

AUTOMATING ROUTINE TASKS: EFFICIENCY ENHANCEMENTS

Automating routine tasks is like setting sails on a windpowered journey; it propels the team forward without requiring constant manual effort. By automating mundane and repetitive tasks, managers free up time for themselves and their team members to focus on more strategic and creative endeavors.

Identifying the right tasks for automation is critical. Not every task should be automated; it's about discerning which processes, when automated, will significantly enhance efficiency and accuracy. This decision-making process is like a doctor determining which medication is best for a particular ailment, considering the benefits and potential side effects.

Implementing automation also requires careful planning and execution. It's not just about setting up the tools but also ensuring they integrate seamlessly into existing workflows and genuinely add value. This integration is akin to introducing a new species into an ecosystem, done thoughtfully to maintain balance and harmony.

In addition, ongoing monitoring and adjustment of automated processes are crucial. Just as a gardener must regularly check and adjust irrigation systems, managers must review automated tasks to ensure they continue to operate effectively and adapt to any changes in the workflow or objectives.

DATA-DRIVEN DECISION-MAKING: UTILIZING ANALYTICS

Data-driven decision-making is comparable to navigating with a compass and an intricate map; it offers a clear, impartial basis for making informed choices. Utilizing data analytics allows managers to cut through ambiguity and base their decisions on concrete evidence and discernible patterns, much like a scientist methodically testing theories and deriving conclusions from the data gathered.

The real power of data-driven decision-making doesn't just come from access to data but also from the skill to interpret and apply it adeptly. Managers must develop a keen analytical sense, like how a chef perfects the art of mixing flavors to create a delicious dish. The more profound their data comprehension, the more accurately it can inform and guide their decisions.

Integrating suitable data analysis tools can significantly enhance this decision-making process. These tools function as advanced magnifying glasses, bringing the subtle details of extensive data into sharp focus, thus enabling managers to base their decisions on comprehensive and detailed insights. These tools are instrumental in sifting through the data to isolate the essential information needed for informed choices.

Furthermore, fostering an organizational culture that consistently collects, analyzes, and acts on data can transform an organization. When team members understand the significance of data in decision-making, they are more likely to participate in and support a data-driven mindset. This atmosphere, akin to a scientific community that relies on empirical evidence, promotes a culture of knowledgeable and efficient decision-making throughout the organization.

REMOTE TEAM MANAGEMENT: VIRTUAL LEADERSHIP

Managing a remote team is like orchestrating a group of musicians not physically present in the same space. It demands a distinctive blend of abilities and tools to sustain communication, unity, and motivation among team members scattered across various locations. Virtual leadership is about fostering a sense of connection and togetherness despite the lack of physical proximity, similar to how a radio show unites listeners from different areas through sound.

Selecting appropriate tools for managing a virtual team is essential. From video conferencing solutions to project management applications, each tool plays a vital role in bridging the physical distance, ensuring that team members stay connected and in sync. This choice is similar to a mechanic carefully selecting the right tools for a specific repair, with each tool fulfilling a distinct and necessary function.

Establishing trust and maintaining consistent communication is crucial in remote team management. Trust forms the bedrock of any team, and in a virtual setting, its importance is amplified. Regular updates, transparent communication, and clear expectations are crucial to fostering and preserving this trust, ensuring the team feels supported and valued despite being geographically dispersed.

Furthermore, prioritizing a balanced work-life dynamic is especially important in remote work scenarios. The blurred lines between office and home life can make it difficult for team members to switch off. Advocating for and demonstrating a balance between professional responsibilities and personal time is like a park offering both sunlit areas for activity and shaded spots for relaxation, providing a harmonious and enjoyable environment for everyone.

STAYING CURRENT WITH TECH TRENDS: CONTINUOUS LEARNING

Keeping pace with technological advancements is similar to a sailor attuning to shifting winds and tides. Today's innovations can quickly become outdated in the fast-evolving realm of technology. For managers, continuous learning and adaptability are essential to harnessing technology effectively for their teams. This dedication to remaining informed mirrors a scholar's commitment to continual study, ensuring their knowledge stays relevant and applicable.

Regular training and professional development are key for managers and their teams to stay informed about the latest tech breakthroughs. This ongoing educational process is like that of a gardener who consistently educates themselves on new gardening methods and plant species, striving to cultivate the finest garden possible.

Additionally, cultivating a culture of curiosity and innovation within the team motivates everyone to stay informed about new technological developments. Encouraging team members to explore and try out new tools can elevate the entire team's ability to integrate beneficial technologies into their work processes. This culture is akin to a laboratory, where experimentation and discovery are integral to everyday activities, fostering continual advancement and growth.

Collaborating with IT specialists and tech gurus can also offer crucial insights into current trends and how they can be effectively implemented within the team's operations. These collaborations are comparable to a student learning from a mentor, where exchanging expertise and experiences significantly enhances the student's understanding and skills.

BALANCING TECH AND HUMAN INTERACTION: HARMONIZING TOOLS AND PEOPLE

Maintaining equilibrium between technology and personal touch is vital in our increasingly digital landscape. Technology can augment efficiency and productivity, but the distinct qualities of human interaction—emotional intelligence, creativity, and empathy—are irreplaceable. Achieving harmony between employing technological tools and nurturing human connections is akin to a musician harmoniously merging electronic and traditional instruments, ensuring the music maintains its essence while incorporating contemporary elements.

Technology needs to complement rather than supplant human interaction. Platforms like video conferencing can simulate face-to-face meetings when direct interactions aren't feasible, yet they should not replace all genuine personal exchanges. The objective is to utilize technology as a conduit to unite individuals, not as a divide that isolates them.

Moreover, discerning when to disengage from digital communication and opting for direct, personal interaction is crucial. Sometimes, a direct conversation, a handwritten note, or a heartfelt gesture can communicate more effectively than any digital correspondence. These personal touches are comparable to sunlight in a garden; while technology can supply some essential elements, nothing can fully substitute the nourishment and warmth that direct sunlight provides.

Training in digital manners and communication is also beneficial for preserving personal connection in virtual interactions. Just as social etiquette governs face-to-face interactions, digital communication has its own best practices promoting clarity, respect, and empathy. Following these guidelines ensures that even in technologically mediated exchanges, the essence of human connection remains vibrant and intact.

Additionally, creating chances for physical meetups, when feasible, can fortify team connections and uplift morale. Organizing team retreats, physical meetings, or social events plays a significant role in cultivating a sense of unity and camaraderie. These gatherings are like family reunions, strengthening the ties and shared experiences that constitute the bedrock of robust, united teams.

MANAGING STRESS AND WORK-LIFE BALANCE

IDENTIFYING STRESSORS: RECOGNIZING TRIGGERS

The first step in managing workplace stress effectively is identifying the various stressors. Much like a detective uncovering clues, this process involves recognizing the factors that contribute to stress, such as excessive workloads, tight deadlines, or interpersonal conflicts. Each team member might have different triggers, making it essential to understand these on an individual basis.

Beyond the obvious triggers, it's also important to be aware of less noticeable stressors like long-term uncertainty or changes in company policies. These can have a subtle yet profound impact on employees' stress levels. Periodic surveys or informal discussions can be instrumental in identifying these hidden stressors.

Understanding the personal life stressors that employees bring to work is also crucial. Personal challenges, such as caregiving responsibilities or health issues, can significantly impact work performance and stress levels. Encouraging a culture where employees feel comfortable sharing these challenges can help address them effectively.

Stressors can also stem from a lack of resources or support in the workplace. This might include inadequate tools to complete tasks or insufficient training, leading to frustration and stress. Regularly assessing the team's resource needs and providing the necessary support can alleviate these stressors.

Finally, it's important to recognize the signs of stress in employees. Changes in behavior, a decrease in productivity, or increased absenteeism can be indicators of stress. Being observant and proactive in addressing these signs can prevent stress from escalating.

TECHNIQUES FOR STRESS MANAGEMENT: COPING STRATEGIES

Effective stress management requires a diverse range of coping strategies. Techniques like time management, prioritization, and delegation can help employees manage their workloads more effectively, reducing stress. Training sessions on these skills can be highly beneficial.

Mindfulness and relaxation techniques such as meditation, deep breathing exercises, or yoga can significantly alleviate stress. Encouraging regular practice of these techniques, possibly through organized sessions, can promote mental well-being in the workplace.

Encouraging physical activity is another effective stress management strategy. Exercise not only improves physical health but also positively impacts mental well-being. Organizing team sports activities or providing gym memberships can be practical ways to promote physical activity among employees.

Creating a support system within the workplace can also help manage stress. This might involve setting up peer support groups, mentoring programs, or providing access to counseling services. Such initiatives create an environment where employees feel supported and less isolated in their stress experiences.

Adopting flexible work policies can also help employees manage stress better. Flexibility in work hours or the option to work remotely can help employees balance their work and personal lives more effectively, reducing the stress associated with rigid work schedules.

ACHIEVING WORK-LIFE HARMONY: BALANCING DEMANDS

Maintaining a healthy equilibrium between professional and personal life is key to mitigating stress and boosting overall well-being. Motivating employees to establish distinct boundaries between their work and personal time is vital to averting burnout. Leaders can set a positive precedent by honoring their own limits and those of their colleagues.

Flexible working conditions can significantly aid in achieving this balance. Providing options such as adaptable working hours or remote working capabilities allows employees to handle their personal commitments better, alleviating the stress of balancing professional duties with their personal lives.

Cultivating an organizational culture that prioritizes work-life balance is fundamental. This means understanding that employees have personal lives that are just as important as their professional ones and respecting this fact contributes to a more contented and efficient team. Acknowledging and honoring personal milestones and responsibilities reinforces this culture.

Offering time management training can further assist employees in finding a suitable work-life balance. Teaching techniques for efficient scheduling, prioritizing tasks, and managing assignments can help employees complete their work more effectively, freeing up time for personal activities.

Encouraging employees to take regular breaks during the workday is also crucial in preventing exhaustion and burnout. Breaks are vital for mental and physical refreshment, allowing employees to return to their tasks with increased energy and concentration.

MINDFULNESS AND RELAXATION: MENTAL HEALTH PRACTICES

Incorporating mindfulness and relaxation techniques into everyday routines can enhance mental well-being and alleviate stress. Engaging in activities such as meditation, guided imagery, or progressive muscle relaxation can offer a peaceful retreat from the ongoing demands of professional life.

Fostering an organizational culture that prioritizes mental health is essential. This may involve offering mindfulness training resources, conducting workshops, or encouraging team members to take brief mindfulness pauses throughout their workday. Such initiatives can sharpen focus, boost productivity, and improve overall mental health.

Additionally, advocating for relaxation practices outside of work can yield positive results. Pursuits like reading, gardening, or other hobbies provide a necessary diversion from job-related stress, allowing employees to rejuvenate and maintain a balanced mental state.

Integrating mindfulness exercises into team gatherings or at the beginning of the workday can establish a serene and positive atmosphere. A short session of guided breathing or mindfulness activities can help center the team, enhancing concentration and collaboration.

Leaders play a crucial role in this aspect and should be attentive to their team's mental health, offering support proactively. This could mean regular check-ins with employees, providing assistance for mental health concerns, or facilitating access to professional mental health services.

SETTING HEALTHY BOUNDARIES: PERSONAL TIME MANAGEMENT

Establishing and upholding clear boundaries is vital for maintaining a healthy balance between professional and personal lives. Employees should be supported in defining and articulating their limits by setting specific hours beyond which they are not expected to engage in work-related communication.

It's important for leaders to honor these boundaries and lead by example. They can avoid sending work emails or making business calls outside of standard working hours, setting a precedent for the entire team.

Educating employees about the significance of boundary-setting can prove advantageous. Offering training sessions or workshops on time management and establishing personal boundaries can equip employees with the necessary skills to better navigate their professional and personal lives.

Encouraging staff to take regular breaks is also key. This includes both brief pauses during the workday and longer periods of leave, like vacations. These breaks are crucial for mental and physical well-being and can help avert burnout.

Furthermore, routinely assessing employee workloads to ensure they are reasonable is crucial for sustaining healthy boundaries. Overloaded employees may struggle to maintain these boundaries, potentially leading to stress and burnout.

AVOIDING BURNOUT: SUSTAINING ENERGY LEVELS

Preventing burnout necessitates active measures and an acute sensitivity to signs of weariness and exhaustion. Managers need to be alert to early indicators of burnout in their team, like diminishing productivity, a drop in engagement, or shifts in behavior and attitudes.

Managing workloads effectively is crucial to averting burnout. This involves a fair allocation of tasks, supplying sufficient resources and support, and establishing achievable deadlines. It's important to ensure employees aren't perpetually overburdened, as this can deplete their energy and dampen their enthusiasm.

Cultivating a workplace culture that emphasizes the importance of regular breaks, vacations, and relaxation time is vital. Motivating employees to take leave for rest and disconnection from work duties is key to preventing prolonged fatigue and burnout.

Encouraging an open dialogue about workloads and stress can aid in pinpointing and tackling potential issues early before they escalate to burnout. It's essential to create a space where employees feel at ease sharing their struggles and seeking support.

Additionally, offering physical and mental health resources, such as wellness programs, fitness facilities, or counseling services, can significantly contribute to avoiding burnout. These supports are instrumental in helping employees maintain their overall health and well-being, which is fundamental for their continuous vigor and productivity.

ENCOURAGING TEAM WELLNESS: COLLECTIVE WELL-BEING

Fostering team wellness means creating a nurturing atmosphere that champions both the physical and mental well-being of team members. Initiatives could range from wellness challenges and health screenings to educational sessions on nutrition and fitness. These endeavors do more than encourage health; they cultivate a sense of unity and shared commitment within the team.

Equally critical is the establishment of policies that bolster mental health. This could entail providing days off specifically for mental health, access to counseling services, or fostering an environment where discussions about mental health are free from judgment or stigma.

Organizing team activities centered around wellness can also boost team spirit and unity. Options like group yoga, mindfulness retreats, or outdoor adventures provide a respite from daily routines and nurture both the mind and body.

Promoting a health-oriented work environment is also key. This includes ergonomic workstations, options for healthy eating, and chances to engage in physical activities during the workday. Such an environment not only supports overall well-being but also helps in mitigating stress and fatigue.

Lastly, acknowledging and celebrating the role of wellness in the workplace underscores its significance. Recognizing team members who make notable progress in their wellness or celebrating achievements in team wellness initiatives not only motivates individuals but also cultivates a culture that values and prioritizes health and well-being.

FOSTERING INNOVATION AND CREATIVITY

CREATING AN INNOVATIVE MINDSET: ENCOURAGING NEW IDEAS

Nurturing an innovative mindset in a team is like tending to a garden brimming with a variety of flourishing plants. It starts with establishing an environment that appreciates and rewards unconventional thinking and challenges existing norms. Leaders are instrumental in this process, actively encouraging their teams to embrace creativity and adopt novel approaches to problem-solving. Consistent brainstorming sessions, public forums for sharing ideas, and acknowledging unconventional thinking can all aid in the cultivation of new ideas.

Integrating creativity into the team's everyday activities is crucial to further promoting this culture of innovation. Allocating time for team members to engage in projects they are passionate about or to delve into new skills and technologies can act as fertile ground for innovative ideas, similar to planting an assortment of seeds to see which ones flourish.

Stimulating curiosity and ongoing learning is also essential. Leaders should champion a culture where asking questions and exploring new avenues are encouraged. Providing opportunities for professional growth, attending industry events, and staying updated with the latest trends can ignite creative thinking.

A mindset conducive to innovation also thrives in an environment where failure is viewed as an opportunity for growth. Leaders should cultivate a safe space where taking calculated risks is not just permitted but encouraged. Understanding that setbacks are integral to the innovation process, much like a scientist considers each experiment a chance to learn, is vital.

Finally, the role of diversity and inclusion in driving innovation cannot be overstated. A team comprising diverse backgrounds, experiences, and perspectives is more likely to generate a wide range of creative ideas. Actively seeking and valuing this diversity is crucial, akin to an artist utilizing a broad spectrum of colors to create a dynamic and vivid masterpiece.

BRAINSTORMING AND IDEATION TECHNIQUES: GENERATING CREATIVITY

Effective brainstorming and ideation act as the creative catalysts within a team, much like a vibrant workshop buzzing with the energy of ongoing innovation. Structured brainstorming sessions can unlock the collective creative genius of the team. Employing strategies such as mind mapping, which visually plots out ideas, or reverse thinking, which flips perspectives, can spark a surge in creative output. Incorporating the SCAMPER method, a technique that prompts users to Substitute, Combine, Adapt, Modify, Put to another use, Eliminate, and Reverse elements within a problem or idea, can further propel divergent thinking, ensuring a rich tapestry of ideas from which to weave the final solution.

Creating an atmosphere where all ideas are welcome during these sessions is important. An environment of non-judgment and openness, like a creative workshop where every contribution is valued, encourages participation and free-flowing creativity. This can be facilitated through exercises that foster empathy and understanding, allowing team members to build on each other's ideas.

Incorporating technology can also enhance brainstorming and creativity. Tools like digital whiteboards or idea management software can capture and organize thoughts, making the process more efficient and inclusive. It's akin to using advanced tools in a workshop to refine and develop raw materials into polished products.

Encouraging solo ideation sessions alongside group brainstorming can also be beneficial. Sometimes, the best ideas come when individuals have the space to think and reflect independently, like an author who finds inspiration in solitude.

Finally, following through on ideas generated in these sessions is crucial. This might involve assigning teams to develop prototypes or conduct feasibility studies. It's about giving ideas the wings to fly and turning creative concepts into tangible innovations.

ENCOURAGING RISK-TAKING: EMBRACING FAILURES AS LEARNING

Fostering a culture of risk-taking in business parallels a ship's captain venturing into unknown seas; it involves seeking new opportunities while being aware of possible dangers. Leaders should cultivate an environment where well-considered risks are endorsed and failures are seen as essential learning opportunities. This mindset creates an atmosphere of innovation where employees feel secure enough to experiment and explore new frontiers.

Leaders can promote risk-taking by leading by example. When those at the helm show readiness to embrace risks and openly discuss the results, regardless of success or failure, they establish a model for the rest of the team. This is like a pioneer demonstrating the merits of exploring untraveled paths.

Allocating resources and supporting pioneering projects, even with uncertain outcomes, is crucial. This may mean dedicating time and budget to research and development or providing mentorship and expert guidance. It's about offering the necessary support for developing ideas and understanding that not all will succeed.

Acknowledging and learning from unsuccessful endeavors is also vital. Organizing 'failure debriefs' where teams dissect what didn't work, and the lessons learned is similar to how the scientific community grows through experimentation. These discussions advance understanding and resilience.

Lastly, it's vital to balance risk-taking with informed decision-making. While innovation is encouraged, it should be aligned with a strategic approach to risk management, ensuring that the risks align with the organization's overarching objectives and principles. This balance is about finding the optimal mix of caution and audacity.

CROSS-FUNCTIONAL COLLABORATION: INTERDEPARTMENTAL SYNERGY

Cross-functional collaboration is a key driver of innovation, like an ecosystem where different species interact to create a dynamic environment. Combining diverse teams from various departments can spark unique solutions that might not emerge in a siloed setting. This collaboration breaks down barriers and encourages the exchange of ideas and perspectives.

Leaders can create mixed teams for specific projects to facilitate this, encouraging members from different functional areas to work together. This is similar to assembling a diverse group of musicians to create a new type of music, blending different styles and instruments.

Encouraging regular interdepartmental meetings and workshops where employees can share their projects and insights fosters a culture of collaboration. These sessions can be like cross-pollination in a garden, where exchanging ideas leads to richer, more diverse outcomes.

Utilizing collaboration tools and platforms can also enhance cross-functional teamwork. In today's digital age, various software can help bridge the gap between different departments, making collaboration more seamless and efficient.

Finally, recognizing and rewarding successful cross-functional collaborations can reinforce their value. This could involve highlighting collaborative achievements in company communications or offering incentives for successful joint projects. It's about celebrating the power of unity in diversity.

REWARDING INNOVATIVE EFFORTS: RECOGNIZING CREATIVITY

Recognizing and rewarding innovative efforts is crucial for cultivating a creative environment. This recognition motivates the individuals involved and signals to the rest of the team that creative thinking and innovation are valued. Leaders can implement recognition programs that highlight and reward innovative ideas and solutions, much like an awards ceremony that celebrates outstanding achievements in art or science.

Financial incentives, while effective, are not the only way to reward innovation. Opportunities for professional development, public acknowledgment, or the chance to lead new projects can also be powerful motivators. It's about understanding what drives each team member and tailoring the rewards accordingly.

Creating a 'hall of fame' for innovative projects or regularly featuring innovative efforts in company communications can also boost morale and encourage a culture of creativity. This public recognition is like a gallery display, showcasing the creative efforts of individuals and teams.

Encouraging peer recognition can also be a powerful tool. When team members acknowledge each other's creative efforts, it fosters a supportive environment where innovation is part of the team's DNA.

Finally, ensuring that the process of rewarding innovation is transparent and fair is crucial. The criteria for recognition should be clear, and all team members should feel they have an equal opportunity to be recognized. This fairness is akin to a sports competition where the rules and judging criteria are transparent and applied equally to all participants.

INNOVATION IN PROCESSES AND PRODUCTS: CONTINUOUS IMPROVEMENT

Innovation should extend beyond just creating new products or services; it should also apply to refining processes and methodologies. Continually enhancing these aspects can result in greater efficiency, improved customer satisfaction, and a competitive advantage. Motivating teams to consistently evaluate and refine their work processes encourages a culture of perpetual innovation.

Leaders can support this by fostering a culture where feedback is actively solicited and appreciated. This might include regular brainstorming sessions aimed at process optimization or implementing systems where employees can propose ideas. It's comparable to a feedback mechanism in machinery, where the output is constantly assessed and fine-tuned for peak performance.

Adopting agile methodologies can further stimulate ongoing innovation. With their focus on flexibility, adaptability, and iterative progress, agile practices are ideally suited to cultivate an environment geared towards continuous improvement.

Inviting teams from different departments to collaborate on process enhancements can introduce new perspectives and creative solutions. This method is similar to cross-pollination in agriculture, where blending different plant varieties yields more resilient and productive results.

Moreover, keeping pace with the latest technological advances and industry best practices can spark ideas for process innovation. Leaders should inspire their teams to stay informed about new trends and technologies that could be integrated into their workflows. This commitment to continuous learning is like an artist who stays updated with the latest artistic methods and styles to enhance their work.

KEEPING A PULSE ON INDUSTRY TRENDS: MARKET AWARENESS

Keeping abreast of industry trends is critical for driving innovation. It's comparable to a navigator using the stars for guidance; staying aware of current market dynamics and foreseeing future developments ensures that a team's efforts align with the wider industry landscape. To remain informed, leaders should motivate their teams to consistently engage with industry-related news, reports, and projections.

Active participation in industry events, such as webinars, forums, and conferences, can offer deep insights into emerging trends and new technologies. These events are platforms for learning from peers, experts, and competitors, similar to explorers exchanging maps and experiences.

Encouraging team members to share insights from these industry events can ignite discussions and inspire innovative ideas. It's like bringing back seeds from uncharted territories that hold the potential to develop new, exciting products or processes.

Collaborating with external entities like universities, research institutions, or other businesses can also offer novel viewpoints on industry trends. These partnerships, like international diplomatic exchanges, can foster mutually advantageous knowledge transfers and spur innovation.

Lastly, cultivating an organizational culture that values flexibility and openness to change is imperative. As industry trends evolve, adapting and embracing new directions becomes crucial for maintaining a competitive edge in innovation. This flexibility is like a ship altering its sails according to shifting winds, ensuring it remains on the right path amidst evolving industry currents.

NAVIGATING ORGANIZATIONAL POLITICS

UNDERSTANDING ORGANIZATIONAL DYNAMICS: POWER STRUCTURES

Navigating organizational dynamics involves an acute understanding of the underlying power structures, akin to a chess player strategizing moves on the board. Recognizing both the formal hierarchy and the informal networks that influence decision-making is essential. Observing interactions and understanding the roles and influences of key stakeholders are critical. Just as a sailor must understand the currents and winds to navigate successfully, a professional must comprehend the power dynamics within their organization.

Understanding the informal networks, often as crucial as the formal structures, requires keen observation and engagement. These networks, like undercurrents, can significantly impact how decisions are made and who holds influence.

Building relationships across various levels and departments can provide insights into these dynamics, like an explorer mapping uncharted territory.

Recognizing one's position within these dynamics is also important. This self-awareness enables individuals to navigate organizational politics effectively, using their understanding of the power structures to inform their actions and decisions. It's akin to a player understanding their pieces' strengths and limitations on a chessboard.

The impact of organizational culture on these dynamics cannot be overlooked. The values, norms, and practices that define the culture also shape the power structures. Understanding this culture is like understanding the rules of a game; it informs how to play effectively and strategically.

Staying adaptable and resilient in the face of shifting power dynamics is crucial. As in any dynamic system, changes in leadership, strategy, or external environment can alter the power landscape. Being able to navigate these changes skillfully is like a navigator adjusting their course in response to changing winds and tides.

BUILDING STRATEGIC ALLIANCES: NETWORKING INTERNALLY

Fostering strategic alliances within an organization is akin to nurturing a diverse and thriving garden. It entails building connections across different departments and hierarchical levels, weaving a supportive and informative network to enhance one's professional endeavors. These alliances are anchored in mutual respect, trust, and a common vision of objectives and goals.

Effective networking often demands venturing beyond one's comfort zone. This means extending outreach beyond immediate colleagues, engaging in cross-departmental projects, and participating in organizational events. This proactive stance in cultivating relationships is similar to planting various seeds, with the potential for some to grow into fruitful alliances.

The depth and authenticity of these connections are crucial. As deeply rooted plants lend stability and sustenance, solid and genuine relationships are more likely to bring lasting benefits. This involves sincere interaction, attentive listening, and a readiness to offer support and aid when necessary.

Strategic alliances are not solely for personal advancement but for reciprocal advantage. It's about discovering complementary strengths and working together towards shared objectives, mirroring the symbiotic relationships found in nature, where each party gains from the collaboration.

Maintaining these alliances calls for continuous effort and care. Regular communication, exchanging pertinent information, and providing assistance are key to sustaining these relationships. Much like garden upkeep, consistent care and attention ensure the enduring growth and vitality of these alliances.

MANAGING UPWARDS: INFLUENCING SENIOR MANAGEMENT

Managing upwards, or effectively influencing senior management, requires a blend of tact, understanding, and strategic communication. It involves understanding the priorities and perspectives of higher-ups and aligning one's initiatives and communications accordingly. Successful upward management is similar to a diplomat who skillfully navigates different interests to achieve a common goal.

Effective communication is critical to managing upwards. It involves presenting ideas clearly, concisely, and in a manner that resonates with senior management's objectives and concerns. This approach is like a translator who accurately conveys the essence of a message in a language that the recipient understands.

Anticipating the needs and expectations of senior management can also facilitate more effective upward management. By proactively addressing these needs, one can demonstrate foresight and initiative, much like a chess player thinking several moves ahead.

Seeking feedback and guidance from senior management is also beneficial. This shows respect for their experience and insight and provides valuable learning opportunities. It's like a student seeking advice from a mentor, keen on understanding and meeting the standards set.

Balancing assertiveness with respect is crucial in managing upwards. It involves confidently presenting one's ideas and viewpoints while being receptive to feedback and willing to adapt. This balance resembles a tightrope walker who skillfully maintains their poise while navigating a high wire.

CONFLICT OF INTEREST AND ETHICS: NAVIGATING MORAL DILEMMAS

Dealing with conflicts of interest and ethical quandaries within an organization can be compared to finding one's way through a complex labyrinth, where each turn presents different ethical challenges. It demands a robust ethical foundation and a steadfast dedication to integrity. Familiarity with the organization's ethics policies and principles is crucial, as they offer a blueprint for navigating ethical decisions.

When a conflict of interest arises, the key lies in transparency and honesty. This entails openly disclosing the conflict to relevant stakeholders and seeking advice on the appropriate course of action. Such forthrightness ensures that decisions are made with the organization's best interests in mind while preserving personal integrity, akin to a judge stepping down from a case to uphold impartiality.

Upholding professionalism and sticking to ethical standards is essential, particularly in testing times. Maintaining ethical principles, even under pressure to bend them, is like a beacon guiding ships through stormy waters.

Recognizing the complexity and subtlety often inherent in ethical dilemmas is important. Navigating these scenarios requires thoughtful deliberation, seeking counsel, and sometimes making hard choices. It's about striking a balance between various conflicting interests and duties.

Cultivating an environment within the organization that champions ethical conduct can also aid in handling these challenges. When ethical behavior is esteemed and consistently promoted, it becomes a fundamental aspect of the organization's ethos, similar to a code of conduct that directs the actions of its community.

CAREER ADVANCEMENT STRATEGIES: NAVIGATING CAREER PATHS

Navigating one's career path within an organization involves strategic planning and foresight. It requires setting clear career goals and understanding the competencies, experiences, and achievements necessary to reach these goals. Like a climber preparing for an ascent, understanding the path and preparing accordingly is key to success.

Seeking mentors and sponsors within the organization can provide invaluable guidance and support in one's career journey. These relationships, like having an experienced guide on a challenging trek, can offer insights, advice, and access to opportunities that might otherwise be unavailable.

Visibility and involvement in high-impact projects can significantly enhance career progression. Much like a performer taking center stage, taking on roles that are critical to the organization's success can lead to greater recognition and advancement opportunities.

Continuously updating one's skills and staying abreast of industry trends are also crucial. This ongoing development is akin to an athlete who continuously trains and improves their technique to stay competitive.

Networking within and outside the organization can open doors to new opportunities and career paths. Building a diverse network is like expanding one's horizons—the broader the network, the more opportunities for learning and advancement.

PERSONAL BRANDING WITHIN THE ORGANIZATION: ESTABLISHING REPUTATION

Developing a strong personal brand within an organization is like creating a distinct and recognizable signature style. It involves consistently demonstrating one's unique skills, contributions, and professional ethos. This personal branding helps establish a reputation as a competent, reliable, and valuable member of the organization.

Effective personal branding requires clearly and consistently communicating one's strengths and achievements. Whether it's through participating in high-profile projects, speaking at company events, or contributing to internal newsletters, each interaction is an opportunity to reinforce one's brand.

Networking, both within and outside the organization, is crucial for personal branding. Engaging with different teams, participating in company-wide initiatives, and being active on professional social media platforms can extend one's reputation beyond one's immediate circle.

Staying true to one's values and maintaining authenticity is crucial to personal branding. It's about building a brand that genuinely reflects one's skills, passions, and beliefs, much like an artist whose work truly expresses their inner world.

Regular self-assessment and adaptation of one's personal brand are also important. As careers evolve and the industry landscape changes, so too should one's brand. This adaptability is like a business that evolves its branding to stay relevant and appealing in a changing market.

RESILIENCE IN POLITICAL ENVIRONMENTS: STAYING TRUE TO VALUES

Maintaining resilience in the complex and often challenging political environments of organizations requires a strong sense of self, clarity about one's values and principles, and the courage to stand by them, even in the face of adversity. Resilience in such environments means not compromising on one's core values for short-term gains or political advantage.

Developing a support network within the organization is key to maintaining resilience. Having colleagues, mentors, or a professional support group who share similar values can provide the necessary backing in challenging times. This support network is a safety net that provides reassurance and strength.

Staying focused on one's goals and objectives is crucial despite the distractions and challenges of organizational politics. It's about maintaining clear vision and direction, much like a sailor keeping their eyes on the horizon amidst turbulent seas.

Adaptability and flexibility in response to changing political dynamics can also aid resilience. Just as a skilled sailor adjusts their sails to the changing winds, a resilient professional adapt their strategies while staying true to their core values.

Lastly, practicing self-care and maintaining a work-life balance are essential for resilience. In the high-stakes environment of organizational politics, taking time for oneself and engaging in activities outside of work can provide the necessary balance and perspective. This self-care is like an athlete resting and recuperating between competitions, ensuring they're ready for the next challenge.

BUILDING AND MANAGING
DIVERSE TEAMS

THE VALUE OF DIVERSITY: BENEFITS AND CHALLENGES

Fostering diversity within a team is like nurturing a garden with an array of different plants; each adds its own distinct beauty and contributes to the overall vitality and richness of the garden. A diverse team offers a wealth of perspectives, experiences, and skills, which can significantly boost creativity and enhance problem-solving capabilities. Similar to how diverse ecosystems are more robust, diverse teams are often better equipped to adapt to changes and tackle intricate challenges.

Yet, managing diversity comes with its challenges. It necessitates an understanding and appreciation of the varied differences, coupled with the ability to weave these diverse perspectives into a unified team strategy.

A key advantage of embracing diversity is the vast array of ideas and solutions it introduces. Teams that welcome diversity tend to outperform their more uniform counterparts, particularly in tasks requiring innovation and creative thinking. Much like an artist's palette with numerous colors, a diverse team has a broader spectrum of options to craft solutions.

However, diversity can also lead to misunderstandings and conflicts if not managed with care. Variances in communication styles, work habits, and cultural norms can potentially lead to friction. It's similar to a conversation involving multiple languages, where the message might get lost in translation without careful navigation.

Ultimately, diversity enriches learning and personal development. Team members exposed to a range of perspectives and experiences can expand their own understanding and cultivate a more empathetic and inclusive outlook. This process is like globetrotting from the comfort of one's space, absorbing insights and viewpoints from each team member's unique experiences and background.

INCLUSIVE LEADERSHIP PRACTICES: FOSTERING BELONGING

Inclusive leadership stands as the foundation of a diverse team, like a pivotal keystone maintaining the integrity of an arch. It entails fostering an atmosphere where every team member is recognized and encouraged to contribute. This requires a deliberate effort to seek and consider diverse perspectives, ensuring every individual's voice is heard and esteemed.

Leaders who are inclusive are adept at active listening and empathy, making a concerted effort to understand the distinct experiences and viewpoints within their team. Their approach mirrors that of a conductor who listens carefully to each instrument, ensuring harmony and that no single sound overwhelms the others.

Facilitating platforms for team members to share their backgrounds and stories can deepen inclusivity. This might take the form of regular team-building exercises or sessions dedicated to cultural exchange. It's comparable to weaving a tapestry, where each strand adds to the overall complexity and beauty of the pattern.

Another critical aspect of inclusive leadership is encouraging and facilitating open and respectful dialogue. This proactive stance ensures that any misunderstandings are addressed quickly and in a manner that builds understanding. It's about establishing norms for interaction that respect and acknowledge every participant's contribution.

Finally, identifying and addressing any instances of exclusion or bias is essential. Inclusive leaders must remain vigilant and proactive in ensuring a safe and supportive environment for all team members, much like a guardian dedicated to the protection and welfare of those they are responsible for.

CROSS-CULTURAL COMPETENCE: UNDERSTANDING DIFFERENCES

Cross-cultural proficiency is crucial when leading diverse teams, similar to how a seasoned traveler adeptly navigates various cultures with respect and insight. It entails recognizing and valuing cultural variances in areas such as communication methods, work ethics, or approaches to problem-solving. Understanding these differences is pivotal for harnessing the strengths inherent in a diverse team.

Acquiring cross-cultural expertise may involve formal education, but it also hinges on a continuous commitment to learning and adapting. This is comparable to a linguist who doesn't just learn multiple languages but also grasps the intricate cultural subtleties associated with each language.

Promoting an exchange of cultural experiences and back-grounds among team members can deepen cross-cultural understanding. Such exchanges can be encouraged in team meetings, cultural celebration days, or casual social events. It's about embracing diversity as a collective educational journey for the entire team.

Addressing language barriers is another key element of cross-cultural competence. When needed, offering language assistance or translation services ensures clear and effective communication among all team members. It's akin to constructing bridges over a river to connect disparate regions.

Additionally, being cognizant and respectful of cultural sensitivities and prohibitions is essential. Such awareness helps avoid miscommunications and cultivates a respectful, harmonious team atmosphere. It's similar to being a mindful traveler who honors local customs and traditions, thus earning the respect and trust of the local community.

MANAGING DIVERSE SKILL SETS: LEVERAGING VARIED TALENTS

Managing a team with diverse skill sets is like orchestrating a symphony where each musician's unique talent contributes to a greater whole. It involves recognizing and leveraging these different skills to enhance team performance and achieve collective goals. This requires an understanding of each team member's strengths and how they can complement each other.

One way to leverage diverse skills is through skill-based task allocation. Assigning tasks based on individual strengths and expertise can lead to more efficient and high-quality outcomes. It's like a coach assigning positions to players based on their unique athletic abilities.

Encouraging cross-functional learning and skill-sharing within the team can also be beneficial. This not only broadens each member's skill set but also fosters a deeper understanding and appreciation of each other's roles. It's like cross-training in sports, where athletes develop various skills to enhance their overall performance.

Creating opportunities for continuous learning and development is also crucial. Providing training, workshops, or mentoring programs can help team members develop new skills and stay abreast of industry trends. It's like nurturing a garden, where continuous care and feeding lead to growth and blooming.

Lastly, celebrating and acknowledging the contributions of team members with diverse skill sets can motivate and encourage further skill development. Recognition of individual talents and contributions reinforces their value to the team, much like a gallery showcasing different artists' unique artworks.

ADDRESSING UNCONSCIOUS BIAS: AWARENESS AND ACTION

Unconscious bias in the workplace can be likened to an undercurrent that subtly but significantly influences decision-making and team dynamics. Addressing these biases requires awareness and deliberate action. It begins with educating oneself and the team about the different forms of unconscious bias and their impact. This education is similar to shining a light on hidden obstacles in a path, making them visible and avoidable.

Encouraging open dialogue about unconscious biases can create an environment where these issues can be addressed constructively. This involves creating safe spaces where team members can share experiences and perspectives on bias without fear of judgment or retribution. It's like opening windows in a stuffy room, allowing fresh air to circulate and clear out stale perspectives.

Implementing structured processes and decision-making criteria can help mitigate unconscious bias's impact. This includes standardized procedures for hiring, promotions, and evaluations. Such structures are like guardrails on a highway, keeping the traffic moving in the right direction and preventing veering off course.

Regularly reviewing and assessing workplace practices and policies for potential biases is also important. This ongoing assessment ensures that biases are identified and addressed promptly, much like a gardener who regularly checks for and removes weeds to maintain a healthy garden.

Encouraging diversity in teams and leadership positions can also help combat unconscious bias. A diverse team is more likely to challenge stereotypical thinking and bring different perspectives to the table, much like a diverse ecosystem that is more resilient and robust.

EQUITY IN OPPORTUNITY AND GROWTH: FAIRNESS IN MANAGEMENT

Fostering equality in opportunities and growth within an organization is like ensuring that every participant in a game has a fair shot at success. It requires crafting a workspace where all employees have equal access to professional development, career progression, and opportunities for growth. This equitable stance guarantees that achievement is determined by talent and effort rather than by one's background or network.

Establishing transparent and impartial processes for promotions, task assignments, and recognitions is vital for nurturing equity. These systems should be grounded in merit and actual performance, ensuring that all employees receive the same evaluations. It's similar to a sports referee who impartially enforces the rules for every player.

Ensuring that all team members have equal opportunities for training and development is also key. This provision makes certain that everyone has the chance to acquire the skills and knowledge needed for career advancement, comparable to giving every student in a class equal access to high-quality educational resources and instruction.

Regularly gathering and addressing employee feedback about equity issues is crucial for identifying and resolving imbalances. Methods like surveys, individual discussions, or group forums can offer insights into employees' perceptions of fairness within the organization.

Finally, mentoring and sponsorship initiatives can significantly aid in advancing equity. These programs can offer additional support and direction to team members from underrepresented or disadvantaged groups, assisting them in more effectively navigating the organizational structure.

CELEBRATING CULTURAL DIFFERENCES: EMBRACING DIVERSITY

Honoring cultural diversity within a team is like orchestrating an international festival where each culture's distinct traditions and customs are celebrated and revered. It's about acknowledging and cherishing the varied cultural backgrounds of team members, viewing this diversity as an asset rather than an obstacle. Embracing cultural differences can strengthen team unity, expand worldviews, and cultivate a more welcoming atmosphere.

Hosting cultural awareness events, having communal meals with dishes from various cultures, or marking different cultural holidays are effective ways to honor diversity. These gatherings offer a platform for team members to exhibit their heritage and learn about others, similar to a cultural exchange program.

Encouraging team members to share their cultural stories and insights can further deepen understanding and respect for diversity. This exchange can occur during team meetings, internal communications, or the organization's social media channels.

Drafting a team charter that explicitly values and respects cultural diversity establishes a clear norm and expectation for conduct. This document acts as a foundational guide, akin to a constitution that outlines the values and principles of a society.

Lastly, acknowledging and respecting the cultural variances in communication styles, work habits, and observance of holidays is crucial. This acknowledgment ensures that every team member feels recognized and appreciated, similar to how a museum respects and highlights art from various cultures, allowing each piece its due significance and space.

PERSONAL BRANDING AND NETWORKING

DEFINING YOUR PERSONAL BRAND: CRAFTING IDENTITY

Defining your personal brand is like painting a self-portrait that encapsulates your appearance, essence, and values. It involves deeply reflecting on what you stand for, your unique strengths, and the distinctive qualities that set you apart. This self-awareness forms the foundation of your professional identity, much like the roots of a tree, anchoring it firmly in the ground and nurturing its growth.

Your personal brand should reflect your career aspirations and values. It's about aligning how you wish to be perceived with your professional goals, akin to a writer choosing a genre and voice that best expresses their message. This alignment ensures that your personal brand resonates with the right audience and opens doors to desired opportunities.

Consistency is key in personal branding. Your actions, communications, and work should consistently reflect your brand. This consistency is like a signature style in art—it makes you recognizable and reinforces your professional identity in the minds of others.

Adapting and evolving your personal brand as your career progresses is also important. Just as an artist's style evolves over time, so should your personal brand. It should be flexible enough to grow and change with you, reflecting your developing skills, experiences, and professional trajectory.

Authenticity in your personal brand is crucial. It should be a true representation of who you are and what you believe in, not a contrived persona. Authenticity fosters trust and credibility, much like a candid photograph captures the true essence of its subject.

EFFECTIVE NETWORKING STRATEGIES: BUILDING CONNECTIONS

Effective networking is like cultivating a garden, where the relationships you grow can bear fruit through opportunities, advice, and support. It's about connecting with others in a way that is mutually beneficial. This involves actively seeking out and participating in events and gatherings where you can meet potential contacts, such as industry conferences, seminars, or local meetups.

Building a diverse network is crucial. Just as a diverse ecosystem is more resilient and vibrant, a diverse network provides a broader range of perspectives, opportunities, and resources. This diversity can be in terms of industry, experience level, background, and skills.

Networking is not just about collecting contacts; it's about building meaningful relationships. This requires follow-up and ongoing engagement, much like nurturing plants requires regular watering and care. Consistent, genuine interactions help in building strong, lasting connections.

Leveraging social media platforms can be a powerful networking tool. Platforms like LinkedIn offer opportunities to connect with professionals worldwide, much like a global networking event. Sharing content, engaging in discussions, and reaching out to professionals with shared interests can expand your network significantly.

Effective networking involves giving as much as you take. Offering help, advice, or resources to your contacts strengthens your relationships. It's about creating a reciprocal network where support flows both ways, much like a symbiotic relationship in nature.

ONLINE PRESENCE AND SOCIAL MEDIA: DIGITAL FOOTPRINT

Your online presence and social media are like a virtual billboard, showcasing your professional brand to the world. It's essential to curate your online profiles so they reflect your personal brand accurately and professionally. This includes maintaining updated profiles on professional networking sites and ensuring that any public social media content aligns with your professional image.

The online content you share and create should add value to your professional narrative. This might involve writing articles, sharing industry news, or commenting on developments in your field. Much like a journalist crafting a compelling story, your online content should engage and inform your audience.

Interacting with other people's content is also an essential part of building your online presence. Engaging with industry leaders, joining professional groups, and participating in online discussions can increase your visibility and establish you as an active professional community member.

Privacy settings and digital etiquette are important considerations. Managing what information is public and understanding the norms of online interactions can prevent potential pitfalls. It's akin to understanding the rules of engagement in a new country—it ensures respectful and appropriate interactions.

Continuously monitoring and updating your online presence is necessary in today's fast-paced digital world. Your online profile is a living document, and regular updates reflect your current interests, achievements, and professional journey, much like a museum that regularly updates its exhibits to reflect current themes and discoveries.

ENGAGING WITH INDUSTRY PEERS: PROFESSIONAL COMMUNITIES

Participating in professional communities within your industry is like being a chorus member, where each individual's contribution enriches the collective harmony. Active involvement in sector-specific groups, associations, or forums opens doors to learning, sharing insights, and keeping up with your area of expertise's latest trends and practices.

Joining industry events, such as conferences, workshops, or seminars, is a fantastic way to network with peers. These gatherings are fertile grounds for idea exchange, relationship building, and potential collaborations. Engaging actively in these events through attendance, presenting, or volunteering can significantly expand your professional network.

Contributing to industry conversations, whether via online platforms, publications, or speaking roles, positions you as an informed and active participant in your field. Like an author adding to a literary genre, your views and knowledge enrich the wider industry dialogue.

Pursuing mentorship within these circles can be immensely rewarding. Whether seeking mentorship or offering it, these relationships offer valuable learning and career guidance comparable to transferring skills and knowledge in an apprenticeship.

Engaging in joint projects or initiatives with industry colleagues can spur innovative solutions and open new doors. These collaborations, similar to business joint ventures, merge the strengths and assets of various individuals to pursue a shared objective.

MENTORSHIP AND SPONSORSHIP: SEEKING AND OFFERING GUIDANCE

Mentorship and sponsorship are critical components of personal and professional development, akin to having a seasoned guide on a challenging journey. Seeking mentors who can offer guidance, advice, and support can accelerate your career growth and broaden your understanding of your industry. It's like having a seasoned traveler who can help you navigate unfamiliar paths and avoid potential pitfalls.

Being a mentor to others is equally important. Sharing your knowledge, experiences, and insights can help others in their career journey while enhancing your leadership and communication skills. It's akin to a teacher who deepens their understanding of a subject by teaching it to others.

Sponsorship involves advocating for another's career advancement or opportunities. As a sponsor, you can open doors for your mentees, recommend them for projects or promotions, and support their professional growth. This role is like a benefactor who invests in an artist's potential, helping them to achieve greater visibility and success.

Developing a mentorship or sponsorship relationship requires clear communication, mutual respect, and a commitment to the growth of both parties. These relationships should be based on trust and a genuine interest in each other's professional success, like a coach and athlete working together towards a common goal.

Active participation in formal mentorship programs or professional organizations can provide structured opportunities for mentorship and sponsorship. These programs are like guided tours; they offer a pathway for connecting and developing these important relationships.

PUBLIC SPEAKING AND PRESENTATION SKILLS: COMMUNICATING EFFECTIVELY

Public speaking and presentation skills are essential tools in your professional arsenal, akin to a craftsman's finely honed tools. Effectively communicating your ideas in meetings, presentations, or conferences can significantly enhance your professional impact. It's about clearly and compellingly conveying your message, much like a storyteller captivates their audience.

Developing these skills often requires practice and feedback. Joining groups like Toastmasters, participating in public speaking workshops, or simply seeking opportunities to speak at work can provide valuable experience. It's akin to a musician rehearsing before a performance, refining their skills through practice.

Understanding your audience is the key to effective communication. Tailoring your message and delivery style to suit your audience, whether they are industry peers, executives, or potential clients, can make your communication more effective. It's like a chef customizing a meal to suit the diners' tastes.

Using storytelling and visual aids can enhance your presentations and speeches. These tools can help illustrate your points more effectively and engage your audience, much like illustrations in a book add depth and interest to the story.

Handling nervousness and maintaining composure during public speaking is also essential. Techniques such as deep breathing, visualization, or practicing mindfulness can help manage anxiety and improve performance. It's like an athlete preparing mentally before a big game, ensuring they are focused and composed.

BUILDING A PROFESSIONAL REPUTATION: TRUST AND CREDIBILITY

Establishing a professional reputation is akin to erecting a robust and striking structure. It's a process that demands time, dedication, and consistent effort. A solid reputation is anchored in trust and credibility, which is cultivated through steady, high-quality performance and ethical conduct. This reputation becomes a defining aspect of your professional identity, earning the recognition and respect of colleagues and others in your industry.

Being dependable and fulfilling commitments is a cornerstone of building trust. Regularly meeting deadlines, honoring your promises, and upholding high standards in your work showcase your reliability, similar to a dependable vehicle known for its consistent performance.

Enhancing your expertise in your area of work also bolsters your reputation. This means engaging in ongoing education, keeping abreast of industry developments, and sharing your knowledge with others. It's comparable to a master artisan who excels in their craft and actively contributes to the growth of their field.

Cultivating strong, respectful professional relationships is another key element. These relationships are like the supportive pillars of a building, reinforcing and elevating your reputation. They form a network of peers who endorse your abilities and character.

Lastly, maintaining integrity and professionalism in all your interactions is crucial. This involves being honest, considerate, and upholding ethical principles. A reputation built upon integrity is formidable, enduring through time and adapting to change, much like a well-constructed fortress.

CONTINUOUS LEARNING AND DEVELOPMENT

LIFELONG LEARNING MINDSET: EMBRACING ONGOING EDUCATION

Adopting a lifelong learning mindset is akin to embarking on an endless journey of exploration and discovery. It involves an ongoing commitment to personal and professional growth and staying curious and open to new knowledge and experiences. This mindset is not just about formal education but encompasses a broad spectrum of learning opportunities, from reading and research to hands-on experiences.

Embracing a variety of learning modalities can enrich this journey. Whether it's attending seminars, engaging in online courses, or participating in interactive workshops, each format offers unique benefits and perspectives. Like a traveler who explores different terrains, a lifelong learner benefits from diverse educational landscapes.

Setting personal learning goals and regularly reviewing these objectives is crucial to maintaining a lifelong learning trajectory. This process is akin to a navigator setting their course and adjusting it as needed. These goals provide direction and motivation, ensuring that the learning journey remains focused and purposeful.

Incorporating learning into daily routines can also enhance the lifelong learning experience. Allocating time for reading industry publications, listening to educational podcasts, or engaging in professional discussions can turn everyday activities into learning opportunities, much like turning a daily walk into an exercise routine.

Lastly, cultivating a network of fellow learners can provide support, inspiration, and a sense of community. Engaging in study groups, attending conferences, or joining professional associations can connect you with like-minded individuals, enriching your learning journey with shared experiences and insights.

SKILLS DEVELOPMENT: EXPANDING CAPABILITIES

Enhancing your skills is similar to an artist continually honing their craft and exploring new artistic methods. In the fast-evolving professional world, it's vital to keep developing and updating your skill set. This could mean delving into advanced technologies, learning new methodologies, or improving soft skills such as communication and leadership.

The first step in skill enhancement is to identify areas where you need growth, like a gardener determining what's needed to enrich their garden. This self-evaluation involves examining your current role, future career goals, and the changing needs of your industry.

Formulating a detailed plan for skill development is crucial. This plan might encompass setting clear, achievable objectives, signing up for relevant courses, or seeking mentorship and coaching. It's about systematically building your abilities, much like constructing a building brick by brick.

Practical experience is often the most effective teacher. Seeking chances to apply new skills in real-world scenarios, be it through new projects, job rotations, or volunteer work, can expedite learning and deepen your understanding, akin to a pilot enhancing their skills through actual flight time.

Imparting your knowledge and expertise to others can reinforce your own learning. Teaching or mentoring in your areas of strength is an excellent way to consolidate your skills while aiding the development of others, similar to an expert artisan teaching their craft to apprentices.

UTILIZING PROFESSIONAL DEVELOPMENT RESOURCES: COURSES AND WORKSHOPS

Leveraging professional development resources, such as courses and workshops, is like adding specialized tools to your toolkit. These resources provide structured learning experiences that can significantly enhance your knowledge and skills. Choosing the right courses and workshops that align with your career goals and learning style is essential.

Online learning platforms have made a vast array of courses and workshops accessible. These platforms offer the flexibility to learn at your own pace and on your own schedule, much like a library that's open 24/7. Whether it's deepening technical skills or exploring new areas like digital marketing or data analysis, these resources provide a wealth of knowledge at your fingertips.

In-person workshops and seminars offer the added benefit of direct interaction with instructors and fellow learners. These settings foster a collaborative learning environment where ideas can be exchanged and discussed, akin to a lively debate where each participant brings a unique perspective.

Staying informed about professional development opportunities offered by your employer or industry associations can also be beneficial. Many organizations provide training programs, sponsor conference attendance, or offer tuition reimbursement for courses relevant to your job, much like a sponsor supporting an athlete's training.

Balancing these structured learning opportunities with on-the-job learning experiences is crucial. Applying what you learn in a practical context can deepen understanding and retention, much like a chef perfecting a recipe through practice.

FEEDBACK AS A LEARNING TOOL: CONSTRUCTIVE CRITICISM

Leveraging feedback as a tool for growth is comparable to using a mirror for personal enhancement. Constructive input from supervisors, colleagues, and mentors offers essential insights into your development areas. Actively seeking and embracing feedback shows a dedication to self-improvement and an openness to change.

Fostering an environment where feedback is routinely exchanged and appreciated is crucial. This might include organizing regular discussions with your manager, engaging in peer reviews, or participating in comprehensive feedback mechanisms like 360-degree evaluations. It's about creating a culture that views feedback as a valuable resource for advancement and learning.

Effectively interpreting and applying feedback is an art. It involves being open-minded, distinguishing between beneficial and non-beneficial critiques, and committing to applying this guidance. Similar to a sculptor who carefully shapes their creation, utilize feedback to refine your professional persona.

It's equally important to balance your own self-reflection with external feedback. Integrating others' viewpoints with your self-awareness ensures that the feedback effectively contributes to your personal and professional growth.

Finally, providing constructive feedback to others can also be enlightening. It aids in developing empathy, honing communication abilities, and gaining a better grasp of team dynamics, akin to a coach who gains as much insight from their team as the team gains from them.

LEARNING FROM INDUSTRY LEADERS: FOLLOWING ROLE MODELS

Learning from industry leaders is akin to following in the footsteps of seasoned explorers. These role models can provide invaluable insights into success strategies, industry trends, and leadership qualities. Observing their career paths, understanding their decision-making processes, and analyzing their successes and failures can offer a blueprint for your own professional journey.

Engaging with the material that these leaders produce, whether through books, articles, podcasts, or interviews, can be very educational. Much like a student learning from master lecturers, absorbing the wisdom and experiences of these leaders can broaden your perspective and inspire innovation.

Attending talks, webinars, or conferences where industry leaders are speaking is another way to learn from them. These events provide opportunities not only to hear their insights but also to ask questions and engage in discussions. It's like attending a masterclass where you can interact with the expert directly.

Networking with industry leaders, when possible, can provide a more personal learning experience. Building connections with these leaders can offer mentorship opportunities and firsthand insights into effective practices and strategies.

Finally, critically analyzing and adapting the lessons from these leaders to fit your own context is important. It's about taking the best of what they offer and molding it to suit your unique situation and career goals, much like an artist who takes inspiration from others but creates their own distinct work.

ADAPTING TO INDUSTRY CHANGES: STAYING RELEVANT

Navigating the rapidly changing professional environment is like traversing constantly evolving landscapes. It calls for adaptability, forward-thinking, and a dedication to lifelong learning. Staying current with industry trends, technological progress, and market shifts is crucial to maintaining competitiveness and effectiveness in your role.

Engaging regularly with industry literature, participating in professional gatherings, and joining relevant forums are key to keeping up-to-date with the latest developments in your field. This continuous involvement is similar to that of a sailor who continually adjusts their sails to the ever-changing winds and currents.

Being receptive to change and open to new methodologies is essential for adapting to industry transformations. This may mean learning new technologies, embracing novel business models, or reevaluating traditional work approaches. It's about being as flexible and adaptable as a tree that sways in the wind to avoid breaking.

Cultivating versatile skills that are applicable in various roles and sectors also contributes to career durability. Abilities like critical thinking, effective communication, and adaptability are timeless, akin to a multi-purpose tool useful in numerous situations.

Actively pursuing opportunities for growth and advancement amid industry changes is important. This proactive approach ensures that you're not merely reacting to changes but actively directing your career trajectory in response to them, similar to a navigator plotting a new course in response to the changing seas.

ENCOURAGING TEAM LEARNING: COLLECTIVE GROWTH

Fostering a culture of learning within your team is like nurturing a thriving ecosystem where each member contributes to and benefits from collective growth. Encouraging team members to pursue learning opportunities, share knowledge, and collaborate on learning projects can enhance the overall skill set and performance of the team.

Implementing regular knowledge-sharing sessions, where team members can present on topics of interest or recent learning, fosters a collaborative learning environment. These sessions can be like a communal garden where everyone brings something to the table, enriching the collective experience.

Encouraging mentorship and peer-to-peer learning within the team can also be beneficial. Pairing more experienced team members with newer ones, or those looking to develop specific skills, can facilitate personalized learning and strengthen team dynamics. It's akin to a guild where craftsmen of different levels work together, sharing skills and knowledge.

Providing access to learning resources, whether through a company library, subscriptions to online courses, or sponsoring attendance at workshops and conferences, is another way to encourage team learning. It's like equipping an expedition team with the tools and maps they need for their journey.

Finally, recognizing and rewarding learning and development efforts can motivate team members to engage in continuous learning. Celebrating these achievements, whether through formal recognition programs or informal acknowledgments, reinforces the value placed on learning and development within the team. It's like applauding actors after a successful performance, acknowledging their effort and skill.

PREPARING FOR ADVANCED LEADERSHIP ROLES

LEADERSHIP SKILL ENHANCEMENT: ADVANCED COMPETENCIES

Preparing for advanced leadership roles involves enhancing your leadership skills to a higher level of sophistication and effectiveness. This progression is similar to an experienced athlete moving into coaching, where the focus shifts from individual performance to guiding others to success. Advanced competencies such as emotional intelligence, advanced decision-making, and strategic conflict resolution become crucial.

Developing a deeper understanding of organizational behavior and change management is essential. As leaders progress, they must master the art of guiding teams through transitions and transformations, akin to a captain steering a ship through turbulent waters.

Cultivating advanced communication skills is also vital. This includes not only conveying ideas effectively but also being adept at listening and understanding the nuances of team dynamics. It's about ensuring that every voice is heard and valued, much like a conductor attuned to every instrument in an orchestra.

Leaders should also focus on enhancing their ability to innovate and drive creativity within their teams. This requires staying abreast of industry trends, encouraging a culture of innovation, and being open to new ideas and approaches.

Finally, honing the skill of resilience is crucial for advanced leadership. The ability to bounce back from setbacks and maintain a steady course in the face of challenges is akin to a seasoned sailor navigating through a storm with calm and determination.

STRATEGIC THINKING AND PLANNING: LONG-TERM VISION

Taking on advanced leadership roles necessitates a highly developed strategic thinking and planning skill set. This skill involves looking beyond immediate concerns and weighing the long-term effects and possible outcomes of decisions. It's comparable to a chess grandmaster who thinks several steps ahead, foreseeing the opponent's moves and strategizing accordingly.

Crafting a clear, far-reaching vision for your team or organization is crucial. This vision should act as a guiding beacon for decision-making and strategic direction, much like how a lighthouse guides ships navigating treacherous waters. The vision needs to be inspiring and attainable, and it should be effectively communicated to all team members.

Leaders in advanced roles must also excel in dissecting complex situations and data to make informed strategic choices. This analytical process resembles a scientist's approach – gathering data, meticulously analyzing it, and drawing reasoned conclusions.

Another critical facet of strategic thinking is balancing long-term objectives with the immediacy of the present. Leaders must adeptly manage current challenges while not losing sight of their long-term goals, akin to maintaining a delicate juggling act where all elements must be kept in motion.

Committing to ongoing education in strategic methodologies, theories, and practices further sharpens a leader's strategic acumen. This continuous educational pursuit is similar to that of an artist who persistently polishes their techniques to perfect their art form.

MANAGING LARGER TEAMS AND PROJECTS: SCALING LEADERSHIP

As leaders advance, they often manage larger teams and more complex projects. This scaling of leadership is akin to a director moving from overseeing a single play to managing an entire theater production. It requires delegating effectively and trusting team members to handle their responsibilities while maintaining oversight of the bigger picture.

Developing robust systems for communication and project management becomes increasingly important. Effective systems ensure that information flows smoothly, tasks are tracked, and progress is monitored, much like a control center coordinating a large-scale operation.

The ability to build, motivate, and maintain a cohesive team culture across larger groups is crucial. Leaders must foster a sense of unity and shared purpose despite the increased team size, much like a mayor fostering a sense of community in a growing city.

Navigating the complexities of larger teams also involves managing diverse personalities, skill sets, and sometimes competing agendas. It requires advanced interpersonal skills and the ability to mediate and align differing viewpoints.

Leaders must also focus on their own time management and prioritization skills as their responsibilities grow. This involves focusing on the most impactful and delegating other tasks, like a general focusing on strategy over individual battles.

EXECUTIVE COMMUNICATION AND INFLUENCE: HIGH-LEVEL INTERACTIONS

In advanced leadership roles, communicating and influencing effectively at an executive level becomes paramount. This involves conveying information clearly and persuasively and understanding the nuances of high-stakes corporate communication. It's like a diplomat engaging in international negotiations, where every word and gesture counts.

Developing a compelling executive presence is crucial. This presence, a blend of confidence, poise, and authenticity, allows leaders to command respect and attention in high-level interactions, much like a seasoned actor captivating an audience.

The ability to tailor communication styles to different audiences is also essential. Leaders must be adept at adjusting their messaging for various stakeholders, from board members to employees, much like a writer who adjusts their tone and style for different genres.

Mastering the art of negotiation and persuasion at this level is crucial. This involves understanding others' motivations and finding common ground, akin to a mediator resolving a complex dispute.

Engaging in active listening and empathy is equally important in executive communication. Understanding and addressing the concerns and viewpoints of others can significantly enhance a leader's influence, much like a therapist who builds trust through empathy and understanding.

NAVIGATING SENIOR MANAGEMENT CHALLENGES: COMPLEX DYNAMICS

Navigating the complex dynamics of senior management involves understanding and managing the intricate web of relationships, power structures, and political undercurrents within an organization. It's like a game of 3D chess, where moves are made on multiple levels and dimensions. Leaders must be adept at understanding these dynamics and maneuvering through them effectively.

Anticipating and managing resistance to change is a common challenge in senior management. Leaders must be skilled in presenting change in a positive light, addressing concerns, and leading teams through transitions, much like a guide leading a group through unfamiliar territory.

Handling high-level conflicts and crises is also a part of senior management. This requires a calm and strategic approach, akin to a captain steering a ship through a storm. Leaders must be able to make tough decisions, communicate effectively during crises, and maintain team morale.

Another challenge is balancing the interests of different stakeholders, from employees to shareholders. Leaders must navigate these often-competing interests, finding a path that aligns with the organization's goals and values, much like a tightrope walker maintaining balance.

Developing a network of trusted advisors and confidantes can be invaluable in navigating these challenges. Like a council of wise advisors, this network can provide diverse perspectives, support, and guidance.

SUCCESSION PLANNING AND MENTORING: FUTURE LEADERSHIP

Succession planning and mentoring are crucial aspects of preparing for advanced leadership roles, akin to planting seeds for the organization's future growth. Leaders must identify and nurture potential successors, ensuring a smooth transition and continuity of leadership. This involves recognizing talent, providing development opportunities, and preparing individuals for future roles.

Mentoring is a key component of succession planning. Leaders should actively mentor promising individuals, sharing knowledge, experience, and insights. This mentorship is like an artisan passing down skills and wisdom to apprentices, ensuring the continuation of craftsmanship.

Involving potential successors in strategic discussions and decision-making processes can provide valuable hands-on experience. It's similar to a pilot allowing a co-pilot to take the controls under supervision, preparing them for future flights.

Succession planning should also thoroughly assess the skills and competencies required for future leadership roles. This assessment ensures that the organization is preparing leaders who are not only capable of handling current challenges but are also equipped for future developments.

Encouraging a culture of leadership development throughout the organization is also essential. This culture ensures that leadership potential is recognized and nurtured at all levels, much like a school that fosters talent in its students from an early age.

VISIONARY LEADERSHIP: INSPIRING BEYOND THE PRESENT

Visionary leadership is a pivotal element in advanced leadership roles, comparable to an architect who conceives of a grand and innovative edifice. It's about transcending present realities to envisage future possibilities. Like a masterful storyteller, a visionary leader captivates and rallies others around a compelling future vision.

A deep comprehension of the organization, its potential, and the wider industry landscape is essential to develop a clear and inspiring vision. It's like an artist who intimately understands their medium and its possibilities, enabling them to craft something truly remarkable.

Effectively communicating this vision in a way that engages and motivates others is key. It involves illustrating a future that is enticing and achievable, similar to how a director vividly brings a script to life, enchanting the audience.

Adaptability is a crucial trait for a visionary leader. Being open to revising the vision based on new insights, feedback, or evolving circumstances is vital. This adaptability can be likened to a skilled navigator who adjusts their course in response to changing weather and sea conditions.

Lastly, embodying the vision in one's own actions and decisions is fundamental. A visionary leader sets an example, manifesting their commitment to the vision and establishing a benchmark for others to emulate, like a pioneer forging a path in unexplored territory.

CONCLUSION

SYNTHESIZING KEY LEARNINGS: REFLECTING ON CORE CONCEPTS

Reflecting on the key learnings from this journey is like looking back at the map of a long and enriching voyage. It involves synthesizing the core concepts that have been explored, from understanding diverse team dynamics to mastering advanced leadership skills. This synthesis helps in forming a cohesive picture of what effective management entails.

The value of effective communication, both within the team and with external stakeholders, stands out as a fundamental learning. It's like the thread that weaves through the management fabric, holding various elements together. Similarly, emotional intelligence in leadership has emerged as a crucial skill, much like the compass that guides a ship—it helps navigate the complex interpersonal aspects of management.

Another key takeaway is the necessity of adaptability and resilience in today's fast-paced business environment. The ability to pivot in response to changing circumstances and to maintain a steady course in the face of challenges is like a sailor adjusting their sails to the shifting winds.

The role of strategic thinking and planning cannot be overstated. It's the blueprint for any successful managerial endeavor, ensuring that decisions are made with a clear, long-term vision in mind. Just as an architect plans a building, a manager must plan their strategies and actions.

Lastly, the significance of continuous learning and development has been a recurring theme. In the world of management, the learning never stops. It's an ongoing process, like a gardener who continually tends to their garden, ensuring it grows and thrives.

PERSONAL GROWTH AS A JOURNEY: EMPHASIZING ONGOING DEVELOPMENT

Personal development in management resembles an ever-continuing journey rather than a final destination. It encompasses a continuous process of growth, self-exploration, and enhancement. Similar to how a traveler accrues new perspectives and experiences on each trip, a manager evolves with each obstacle navigated and triumph achieved.

This journey necessitates a dedication to self-betterment and a readiness to venture beyond familiar boundaries. It involves an ongoing quest for new knowledge, skills, and experiences reminiscent of an explorer consistently seeking new vistas. This approach ensures that managers remain dynamic and proficient in their roles.

Integrating lessons from failures is a critical component of this growth path. Every challenge is a chance to learn and advance, much like an artist who refines their artistry with each brushstroke.

Welcoming feedback and being receptive to constructive criticism is essential for personal development. It's about recognizing feedback as a crucial instrument for enhancement, similar to a mirror offering a clear reflection that guides self-improvement.

Finally, personal growth entails balancing professional advancement and personal well-being. It's crucial to prioritize self-care, ensuring the quest for professional success does not undermine personal health and happiness. This equilibrium is comparable to a musician ensuring the perfect blend of rhythm and melody in their music.

IMPLEMENTING STRATEGIES IN REAL-WORLD SCENARIOS: PRACTICAL APPLICATION

Translating learned strategies and concepts into real-world practice is the essence of proficient management. It's the transition from theoretical understanding to practical execution, akin to an actor finally performing live after extensive rehearsals. This translation necessitates tailoring the learned approaches to the unique dynamics, challenges, and opportunities of one's specific organizational and team environment.

A pragmatic and adaptable approach is essential when applying these strategies. Given that each team and scenario is distinct, a method effective in one setting might not suit another. It's comparable to a chef who tweaks their recipe to suit their diners' available ingredients and taste preferences.

Incorporating team collaboration and input can significantly enhance the application of these strategies. It involves tapping into the collective knowledge and experience of the team, much like a conductor blends musicians' individual contributions to create a harmonious symphony.

Assessing the effectiveness of implemented strategies is equally vital. This assessment entails establishing clear success metrics and being prepared to modify the strategy as required. It's similar to a navigator who continually checks and adjusts their path to ensure they're on course to their destination.

Lastly, documenting and reflecting on the outcomes of these applied strategies is critical for ongoing improvement. Maintaining a record of what succeeded and what didn't offers valuable insights for future initiatives, akin to a scientist meticulously noting experiment results to guide further research.

THE NEXT STEPS FOR NEW MANAGERS: FUTURE CHALLENGES

As new managers embark on their professional journey, they face a path brimming with both opportunities and challenges. The immediate task at hand is to apply their acquired knowledge to their current roles while also gearing up for future responsibilities. This phase is about building upon the established groundwork and approaching the future with both confidence and eager anticipation.

Actively seeking out new challenges and growth opportunities is essential for these managers. This proactive stance helps them remain enthusiastic, motivated, and dynamic in their roles, similar to an athlete who constantly seeks new competitions to hone and showcase their skills.

Cultivating and maintaining relationships within the organization is another critical aspect. These connections, from team members to other key stakeholders, are vital for effective management and leadership. They act as a support system, offering insights and opportunities akin to a network of roads linking various parts of a city.

Staying informed about industry trends and developments is also crucial for new managers. In a rapidly evolving business world, staying knowledgeable is key to making well-informed decisions and staying ahead of the curve, much like a sailor who keeps updated about changing weather and sea conditions.

Finally, preparing for future leadership roles encompasses not only personal advancement but also the development of others. It's about mentoring and supporting team members, ensuring the perpetuation of a culture of learning and growth reminiscent of a teacher who imparts knowledge while inspiring students to become educators themselves.

BUILDING A SUPPORTIVE NETWORK: LEVERAGING RELATIONSHIPS

Building a supportive network is like weaving a safety net that can catch and support you throughout your managerial journey. This network includes colleagues, mentors, industry peers, and other professional connections. Nurturing these relationships is essential for support, advice, and opportunities.

A supportive network provides a sounding board for ideas and challenges. Like a council of advisors, this network can offer diverse perspectives and wisdom, helping you navigate complex decisions and situations.

Actively engaging in professional communities through associations, online forums, or local groups can expand your network. This engagement is like planting seeds in different gardens, increasing the chances of growth and connection.

Reciprocity is key to building a supportive network. It's about offering support and assistance as much as seeking it. This mutual exchange strengthens relationships and creates a culture of support and collaboration, like in a community where members look out for each other.

Maintaining and nurturing these relationships over time is crucial. Regular check-ins, sharing updates, and celebrating successes together keep the network strong and active, much like tending to a garden to ensure it continues to flourish.

STAYING INSPIRED AND MOTIVATED: SUSTAINING MOMENTUM

Staying inspired and motivated as a manager is like keeping the flame of a lantern burning brightly. It involves continually finding sources of inspiration and motivation, whether from personal goals, your team's success, or your work's impact. Keeping this flame alive ensures you remain passionate and driven in your role.

Setting personal and professional goals can provide direction and motivation. These goals, like milestones on a journey, offer a sense of purpose and achievement as you progress. Celebrating these achievements, no matter how small, can also boost motivation and morale.

Finding inspiration from role models, industry leaders, or successful figures can also motivate you. Their stories and achievements can provide encouragement and a blueprint for success, like a map that guides explorers to their destination.

Maintaining a healthy work-life balance is essential for sustained motivation. Taking time for personal interests and hobbies is important, ensuring that you recharge and prevent burnout. This balance is like a musician playing for passion and performance, ensuring they remain inspired and engaged.

Remaining open to new experiences and challenges can renew motivation and provide fresh perspectives. It's about embracing change and seeing it as an opportunity for growth and learning, much like an adventurer eagerly anticipating new adventures.

FINAL THOUGHTS AND ENCOURAGEMENT: A MESSAGE OF HOPE

As we reach the end of this book, it's time to reflect on the strides made and look forward with eager anticipation. The journey of mastering management and leadership is a perpetual one, constantly evolving. Much like a river that flows ceaselessly, shaping new paths, your path in management is replete with limitless prospects for advancement and learning.

Face forthcoming challenges with assurance and a positive outlook. Each obstacle is a hidden opportunity to learn, evolve, and refine your leadership skills. It's about perceiving every situation as brimming with potential and promise.

Trust in your capacity to effect change. Your leadership has the power to inspire, catalyze positive transformation, and propel success. Just as a lighthouse steers ships safely to shore, your guidance can illuminate the way for your team, providing direction and encouragement.

Maintain your commitment to lifelong learning and self-improvement. The management realm is ever-changing, offering continuous opportunities for growth and exploration. Let your innate curiosity and zeal for knowledge drive you like an adventurer drawn to the unknown.

And lastly, remember that this journey is not a solitary one. There is a network of friends, colleagues, and mentors by your side. Together, you can tackle the intricacies of management and leadership, much like a crew collaboratively navigating a ship across a vast, sometimes tumultuous, oceanic expanse. Armed with determination, resilience, and optimism, the future holds endless potential and bright prospects.

SUGGESTED READINGS

Bennis, Warren - "On Becoming a Leader"

Blanchard, Kenneth H. - "The One Minute Manager"

Carnegie, Dale - "How to Win Friends and Influence People"

Collins, Jim - "Good to Great: Why Some Companies Make the Leap... and Others Don't"

Drucker, Peter F. - "The Effective Executive: The Definitive Guide to Getting the Right Things Done"

Duhigg, Charles - "Smarter Faster Better: The Secrets of Being Productive in Life and Business"

Ferrazzi, Keith - "Never Eat Alone: And Other Secrets to Success, One Relationship at a Time"

Gladwell, Malcolm - "Outliers: The Story of Success"

Goldsmith, Marshall - "What Got You Here Won't Get You There: How Successful People Become Even More Successful"

Heath, Chip & Dan Heath - "Switch: How to Change Things When Change Is Hard"

Kouzes, James M. & Barry Z. Posner - "The Leadership Challenge: How to Make Extraordinary Things Happen in Organizations"

Pink, Daniel H. - "Drive: The Surprising Truth About What Motivates Us"

Rath, Tom - "StrengthsFinder 2.0"

Robbins, Tony - "Awaken the Giant Within: How to Take Immediate Control of Your Mental, Emotional, Physical and Financial Destiny!"

Sandberg, Sheryl - "Lean In: Women, Work, and the Will to Lead"

Sinek, Simon - "Start with Why: How Great Leaders Inspire Everyone to Take Action"

Stanley, Andy - "Next Generation Leader: 5 Essentials for Those Who Will Shape the Future"

Tracy, Brian - "Eat That Frog!: 21 Great Ways to Stop Procrastinating and Get More Done in Less Time"

Wakeman, Cy - "No Ego: How Leaders Can Cut the Cost of Workplace Drama, End Entitlement, and Drive Big Results"

Zenger, John H. & Joseph Folkman - "The Extraordinary Leader: Turning Good Managers into Great Leaders"